READING MATTHEW FOR THE FIRST TIME

Wilfrid J. Harrington, OP

Paulist Press
New York / Mahwah, NJ

Cover image by Renata Sedmakova / Shutterstock.com

Cover and book design by Sharyn Banks

Library of Congress Cataloging-in-Publication Data

Harrington, Wilfrid J.
Reading Matthew for the first time / Wilfrid J. Harrington, OP.
pages cm
Includes bibliographical references.
ISBN 978-0-8091-4853-0 (alk. paper) — ISBN 978-1-58768-327-5
1. Bible. Matthew—Criticism, interpretation, etc. I. Title.
BS2575.52.H375 2014
226.2`06—dc23

2014006426

ISBN 978-0-8091-4853-0 (paperback)
ISBN 978-1-58768-327-5 (e-book)

Published by Paulist Press
997 Macarthur Boulevard
Mahwah, New Jersey 07430

www.paulistpress.com

Printed and bound in the
United States of America

CONTENTS

Introduction

The Synoptic Gospels are notably similar; all the more reason that their distinctive differences underline the individuality of the three evangelists. In this trio, we have evidence of the pluralism of New Testament theology and, more specifically, of its Christology. Mark, Matthew, and Luke are Christian theologians. They do not speak with one "official" voice. They witness convincingly to the richness of Jesus Christ and the power of his message. Matthew's portrait of Jesus is colored by two factors: he is a committed Jewish-Christian, wholly convinced that Jesus is the Messiah—the Christ—of Jewish hope and expectation; furthermore, he is grieved by the antagonism of contemporary Judaism.

The center of Matthew's Gospel—the public ministry of Jesus—is built of five major sections, each with a pattern of narrative-plus-discourse (chapters 3—25). Added to this center core is the Infancy Narrative (chapters 1—2) and the Passion Narrative (chapters 26—27), which form the prologue or introduction and the conclusion or climax respectively. This Gospel is, before all else, a proclamation of Jesus of Nazareth, risen Lord, present and active in the Christian community. Matthew acknowledges Jesus as Prophet and Healer. However, what separates him from the other synoptists is his emphasis on Jesus as Teacher or Sage.

In the stressful days after the traumatic disaster of AD 70 (the destruction of Jerusalem), Matthew's community found themselves in a state of "cold war" with official Judaism. The community's stance is that Jesus is the Teacher who speaks more authoritatively than Moses. This is emphasized by Matthew throughout the five discourses or sermons in which the Teacher proclaims his message. It is not the evangelist's whole story, but it grants us entry into the heart of his proclamation.

In his Infancy Narrative (chapters 1—2), Matthew asserts firmly that Jesus is son of David and son of Abraham: Savior of Jew and Gentile. In the Sermon on the Mount (chapters 5—7), Jesus addressed his people, assuring them that he had not come to abolish the Torah and the Prophets, but rather that he was their prophetic fulfillment. For the Christian, the ultimate authority is his word. Jesus spoke in parables and, in the Sermon in Parables (chapter 13), Matthew's preoccupation with the struggle with contemporary Judaism is evident. The Sermon on the Church (chapter 18) outlines the characteristics of leadership in a Christian community—marked by special care for the weak and the vulnerable. Its exercise should carry the stamp of service, whereby the members of the community display mutual concern. The Judgment Sermon (chapters 24—25) focuses on eschatological trials, but with a regard for the tribulations of Christians in the present.

The Gospel ends with the passion, death, and resurrection of Christ (chapters 26—28). The infant Emmanuel—God-with-us—of chapter 1:23 is now the risen Lord who promises to be with us to the end of the age (28:20). For Matthew, Jesus is now the presence of God in the world. The story has come full circle, but it does not end here. There is the ongoing Christian task: "Go therefore and make disciples of all nations" (Matt 28:19).

CHAPTER 1

Overview

> ***Every scribe who has been trained for the kingdom of heaven is like a master of a household who brings out of his treasure what is new and what is old.***
>
> Matthew 13:52

In the decade AD 80–90, a Jewish Christian theologian—we name him Matthew—made a synthesis of Mark and a source known as *Q*, which is considered to be a collection of Jesus' sayings and parables. In addition, he had access to other material conventionally designated *M*. His community, possibly based in Antioch, located in present day Turkey near the border with Syria, was in a crisis situation. It had been a wholly Jewish community. But now, after the destruction of Jerusalem in AD 70 and the reorganization of a shattered Judaism, the community has broken with official Judaism. As a Jewish Christian writing out of and for a largely Jewish Christian community, Matthew, like all Jews, had to confront the radical challenge of his Jewish identity. Difficult and stark questions were raised: Where is Israel now? Who is heir to the biblical promises? Before addressing these questions, we must first note that the Jewish response was two-pronged: apocalyptic and early rabbinic (formative) Judaism.

APOCALYPTIC JUDAISM

It is generally assumed that apocalyptic Judaism sprang from the experience of alienation, or that it arose in a time of crisis—either perceived or real. Such an apocalyptic group sets up its own symbolic universe or worldview: a system of thought within which it can live. Usually, it does so out of protest against the dominant society with which it is in conflict. The group has a painful experience of alienation, which may be due to a quarrel with the power-group within its own society.

Such was the situation of Matthew's community. Originally an exclusive Jewish-Christian group, they were alienated from their ethnic brothers and sisters and involved in a "civil war," which explains the sad virulence of chapter 23. The tragedy is that here, as with depressing regularity throughout "Christian" history, Jesus was dragged into Christian and political disputes.

Two major Jewish apocalypses responded to the AD 70 crisis: 4 Ezra and 2 Baruch—both dating from about the same time as Matthew and both acknowledging Roman victory. Their verdict is that the victory is ephemeral and that God will have the last word. His Messiah will emerge soon to reverse the present tragic state of Zion.

FORMATIVE JUDAISM

The apocalyptic view was bolstered by another response. Vindication was certain, but it had to be prepared for and might be hastened by faithful observance of the Law, the revelation of God's will. Hence, the contribution of another movement after AD 70, which was formative of subsequent Judaism. The three pillars of Israel had been Torah, temple, and land. Now that land and temple had gone, it was Torah alone that remained. The Pharisees, who had been stalwart champions of Torah, now came into their own. In their view, loyal and total observance of Torah was the way of hope and the only adequate response to the crisis. Only by way of meticulous observance of the Law could God's promises to his people be fulfilled. When the way had been prepared, God's Anointed One would appear to restore the fortunes of Zion. As Daniel Harrington describes:

> Matthew shared the apocalyptic hope of 4 Ezra and 2 Baruch. But Matthew identified the Messiah as Jesus of Nazareth and took Jesus' interpretation of the Law as the proper guide to behavior in the present. Matthew shared the practical agenda of formative Judaism on many points. But he rejected the Pharisees' traditions and interpretation in favor of the teachings of Jesus. Thus Matthew's Gospel emerges as a Jewish Christian response to the events of 70 AD.[1]

MATTHEW

The Jewish Christian, Matthew, wrote a Christian Gospel. For him, as for Paul, the hope of Israel was in Jesus Christ. His post-AD 70 situation was not that of Paul, who was wholly convinced that Israel had not been, because it never could be set aside (cf. Rom 9–11).

Immersed in the conflict situation after AD 70, Matthew was not so sanguine. For him, official Judaism was the enemy. With the powerful priesthood having been obliterated, the Pharisees were his target—his *bête noir*. His polemical stance is understandable in the context of his situation, and taken out of context, it proves disastrous. Chapter 23, above all, has led to nearly a universal Christian characterization of Pharisees as "hypocrites," which is grossly unfair. Furthermore, that seeming self-curse, "His blood be on us and on our children" (27:25), has occasioned brutal persecution of Jews throughout Christian history. Unfortunately, there has been a sad failing in perception. While in Matthew's situation, ethnic Jews—Christian and non-Christian—were in conflict, such conflict is not anti-Semitic.

The Matthean community was probably predominantly Jewish Christian, but would have also had a notable Gentile component. It is likely that the initial exclusively Jewish Christian community would, at that stage, have seen its mission as addressed to fellow Jews. With the failure of this venture (cf. 11:20–24; 23:37–39; 28:15), there was an increasing effort to reach the Gentiles (cf. 12:21; 13:38a; 24:9–14; 26:13), which would then have opened the mission to the whole world. Matthew's view is expressed in 24:14: "And this good news of the kingdom will be proclaimed throughout the world, as a testimony to all the nations; and then the end will come."

The change in focus from Israel to a universal perspective could not have happened without tension. This is manifest in the contrast of the declarations: "Go nowhere among the Gentiles, and enter no town of the Samaritans, but go rather to the lost sheep of the house of Israel" (10:5b–6; 15:24) and "Go therefore and make disciples of all nations" (24:19). In one, the speaker is the earthly Jesus, in the other the risen Lord. The discrepancy may reflect an initial hesitation at a wider outreach followed by the ultimate embrace of a universal mission.

Nevertheless, the universal mission is present from the start of Matthew's Gospel. In the genealogy, Jesus is "son of Abraham" (1:1). As such, he is the fulfillment of the promise that through Abraham "all the nations of the earth" would be blessed. The first citation of Scripture, "and they shall name him Emmanuel, which means, 'God is with us'" (1:23), forms an inclusion with the promise in 28:20: "And remember, I am with you always, to the end of the age." The inclusion is decisive for understanding the Gospel of Matthew: Jesus' way represents the way of God to the nations.

CHURCH

In the context of mission, note that Matthew displays a deeper interest in the church than any of the other evangelists.

He alone uses the word *ekklesia*, meaning "assembly" or "church" (16:18; 18:17). The narrative section, Matthew 11—12, opens with a question of the Baptist: "Are you the one who is to come, or do we wait for another?" (11:3). The evangelist expects his readers to ask themselves the same question. And yet Matthew believed that a decision regarding Jesus necessarily involved a decision regarding his church, and authentic commitment to Jesus was possible only within the context of membership in his community.

Matthew sees "church" primarily in terms of discipleship. For him, the church is a community formed by those who have heard Jesus' call to follow him. Indeed, in his Gospel it becomes difficult to distinguish between the disciples and the community (or church) because for Matthew they blend together. Jesus' disciples become a model for the Matthean community, which discerns in them patterns of faith to be lived out in all its aspects and recognize a call to the universal mission.

SOURCES

The majority of New Testament scholars support the Two-Source Theory: Mark is the earliest Gospel; Matthew and Luke have used Mark and another hypothetical text known as Q (from the German *Quelle*, "source"). The theory accounts reasonably for the large amount of material shared by Matthew and Luke. Additionally, each evangelist has material proper to himself: for instance, the Infancy Narratives (Matt 1—2; Luke 1—2). The source Q is thought to be a

Greek document containing almost entirely a collection of sayings and parables of Jesus. The outline of this document is found persuasively in Luke. Its tone is strongly sapiential with a notable eschatological emphasis.

By including elements of Q, Matthew has highlighted the teaching role of Jesus. Of course, while the hypothetical Q document is not extant, this has not hindered some scholars from presenting assured reconstructions, nor indeed from describing the Q community with a confident sketch of its theology. Regardless, the existence of a Q document provides the best explanation for the remarkable non-Markan connections between Matthew and Luke.

STRUCTURE

Matthew might be characterized as a literary architect. After the prologue (chapters 1—2), the public ministry of Jesus is welded into five sections, each section comprising narrative and then discourse—the five discourses form the pillars of the Gospel.

The Gospel of Matthew falls naturally into seven parts: the first part, the Infancy Narrative (chapters 1—2), forming a prologue, and the seventh part, the Passion Narrative (chapters 26—28), forming a climax or epilogue. The structure of chapters 3—25 is precise: five sections, each containing a narrative section and a discourse. Each of the discourses has a brief introduction (5:1–2; 10:1–5; 13:1–3; 18:1–2; 24:1–3), and each is closed by a stereotypical formula: "And it came to pass, when Jesus had finished these sayings…" (7:28; 11:1; 13:53; 19:1; 24:1—3). These five central parts of the Gospel are not many disconnected units, but rather are closely linked. The narratives indicate the progressive movement of events, while the discourses illustrate a parallel progress in the messianic concept of the kingdom of heaven.

The Plan

I. Prologue: Infancy Narrative (1—2)

II. Proclamation of the Kingdom (3—7)
- The Mission Begins (3—4)
- Sermon on the Mount (5—7)

II. Mission in Galilee (8:1—11:1)
- Miracle Stories (8—9)
- Mission Sermon (10:1—11:1)

III. Opposition from Israel (11:2—13:53)
- Opposition and Response (11:2—12:50)
- Sermon in Parables (13:1–53)

IV. The Kingdom Develops (13:54—18:35)
- Formation of Disciples (14—17)
- Sermon on the Church (18)

V. Towards the Passion (19—25)
- Mounting Opposition (19—23)
- Judgment Sermon (24—25)

VI. Climax: Passion, Death, and Resurrection (26—28)

In the discourses or sermons, a concentric pattern is discernible:

1. **Sermon on the Mount**
2. **Mission Sermon**
3. **Sermon in Parables**
4. **Sermon on the Church**
5. **Judgment Sermon**

In this pattern, (1) corresponds to (5); (2) corresponds to (4), and the central sermon (3) takes on special significance. Furthermore, the couplets (1) and (5) and (2) and (4) should be read in such a manner that they throw light on each other. Given this pattern, it could be inferred that the Gospel was constructed on a concentric model and that the structure indicates that the evangelist intended the title "son of Abraham" given to Jesus in the prologue (1:1) to be related to the command given to the Eleven in the epilogue: "Go therefore and make disciples of all nations." Jesus is the realization of the promise made to Abraham: "In you all the families of the earth shall be blessed" (Gen 12:3). We have here an evident stress on the universality of salvation. It has a place of high priority in the theological perspective of Matthew, as is shown by its exposed position at the very beginning and end of the Gospel.

LITERARY FEATURES

Reflection Quotations

While structure is the dominant literary feature of Matthew's Gospel, another distinctive feature is his use of "reflection" or "formula" quotations, which sit loosely in their context. If removed, they would not be missed. The evangelist is sure that Jesus is fulfilling a divine purpose, a purpose articulated in the prophetic word. Accordingly, he has recognized the applicability of particular Old Testament texts to particular incidents in Jesus' life. There is some uncertainty as to the precise number of quotations that are notably present in the Infancy Narrative (chapters 1—2). Here is a widely accepted list of them.

1. 1:22–23: *All this took place to fulfill what had been spoken by the Lord through the prophet: "Look, the virgin shall conceive and bear a son, and they shall name him Emmanuel," which means, "God is with us."* (cf. Isa 7:14)

   We are told that the virginally conceived Jesus is God-with-us, the very presence of God himself. It is by removing sin from his people that Jesus ("he will save his people from their sins", v. 21) makes God present among his people.

2. 2:5–6: *They told [Herod], "In Bethlehem of Judea; for so it has been written by the prophet: 'And you, Bethlehem, in the land of Judah, are by no means least*

among the rulers of Judah, for from you shall come a ruler who is shepherd of my people Israel.'" (cf. Micah 5:2)

Jesus, son of David (Matt 1:1), was born in Bethlehem, the birthplace of David.

3. 2:14–15: *Then Joseph got up, took the child and his mother by night, and went to Egypt, and remained there until the death of Herod. This was to fulfill what had been spoken by the Lord through the prophet, "Out of Egypt I have called my son."* (cf. Hosea 11:1)

   Jesus is "my son"—Son of God. In being called out of Egypt, he reenacted the Exodus event of his people.

4. 2:17–18: *Then was fulfilled what had been spoken through the prophet Jeremiah: "A voice was heard in Ramah, wailing and loud lamentation, Rachel weeping for her children; she refused to be consoled, because they are no more."* (cf. Jer 31:15)

   Ramah is the place of Rachel's death and the place where the deportees were assembled for the journey to exile in Babylon. Symbolically, Jesus suffered the exile of his people.

5. 2:23: *There he made his home in a town called Nazareth, so that what had been spoken through the prophets might be fulfilled, "He shall be called a Nazorean."*

   Here, the alleged scripture quotation is nowhere attested, and Nazareth is not mentioned in the Old Testament. It was Matthew's conviction that, if it were scripturally appropriate that Jesus was born in Bethlehem, then it had to be scripturally appropriate that his home was Nazareth.

6. 4:13–16: *He left Nazareth and made his home in Capernaum by the sea, in the territory of Zebulum and Naphtali, so that what had been spoken through the prophet Isaiah might be fulfilled: "Land of Zebulum, land of Naphtali, on the road by the sea, across the Jordan, Galilee of the Gentiles—the people who sat in darkness have seen a great light, and for those who sat in the region and shadow of death light has dawned."* (cf. Isa 9:1–2)

   Jesus' return to Galilee from the "wilderness" (Matt 4:1–11) after John's arrest (4:12) was in accordance with God's will. He took on himself the mission of the Baptist.

7. 8:16–17: *That evening they brought to him many who were possessed with demons; and he cast out the spirits with a word, and cured all who were sick. This was to fulfill what had been spoken through the prophet Isaiah, "He took our infirmities and bore our diseases."* (Cf. Isa 53:4)

   The text from Isaiah speaks of a vicarious sacrificial death. Matthew was well aware that Jesus was the suffering servant who redeemed us by his death (vv. 20:28; 26:28). Here he combines Jesus' healings with his role of servanthood. His miracles are related to his passion; they are part of his redeeming work.

8. 12:14–21: *The Pharisees went out and conspired against him, how to destroy him. When Jesus became aware of this he departed. Many crowds followed him, and he cured them, and he ordered them not to make him known. This was to fulfill what had been spoken through the prophet Isaiah: "Here is my servant, whom I have chosen, my beloved, with whom my soul is well pleased. I will put my Spirit upon him, and he will proclaim justice to the Gentiles. He will not wrangle or cry aloud, nor will anyone hear his voice in the streets. He will not break a bruised reed or quench a smoldering wick until he brings justice to victory. And in his name the Gentiles will hope."* (cf. Isa 42:1–4)

The text from Isaiah is used by Matthew to explain why Jesus withdrew from the synagogue of the Pharisees (see Matt 12:9) and why he deliberately avoided making his true identity public: this is how God's meek and humble servant-son operates. (The Greek *pais* can mean both "servant" and "son"). John Meier has a splendid commentary: "It is this servant-son who will proclaim God's just yet saving will (justice) to the pagans. Since Jesus has been forced to withdraw from 'their synagogue' because of the Pharisees' deadly hatred, the prophetic reference to the Gentile mission is fitting. Because Israel will fail to accept Jesus' proclamation of salvation, the gospel will be directed to the Gentiles. In the face of this hatred from his own people, Jesus does not reply with vengeful wrath or strident arguments (cf. 5:38–48). The meek servant seeks not publicity for himself but healing for others. Those broken in body or depressed in spirit (the reed and the wick) receive from him not the *coup de grace* but recovery. In the teeth of opposition he will continue this mission, even on the sabbath, till he sees God's will victorious in the death-resurrection. From that moment on, the pagans will be able to place their hope in his name i.e. in his person as revealed and preached to them (cf. 'name' in 28:19). This triumph of Jesus will come about not through military might but through the meekness, even humiliation and death, of the servant who sacrifices himself to heal others."[2]

9. 13:34–35: *Jesus told the crowds all these things in parables; without a parable he told them nothing. This was to fulfill what had been spoken through the prophet: "I will open my mouth to speak in parables; I will proclaim what has been hidden from the foundation of the world."* (Ps 78:2)

The quotation from a psalm indicates that Matthew evidently takes a broad view of "prophet." The discourse in parables is fulfillment of prophecy. This passage marks a turning point in the Parable Sermon of chapter 13: Jesus turns from the crowds to his disciples (v. 36). The "crowds" represent unbelieving Judaism. For them, the message of

Jesus is a "parable" in its enigmatic form of speech ("hidden"). What is hidden will be revealed to those who are open to receive (13:36–52).

10. 21:4–5: *This took place to fulfill what had been spoken through the prophet, saying: "Tell the daughter of Zion, Look, your king is coming to you, humble, and mounted on a donkey, and on a colt, the foal of a donkey."* (cf. Isa 62:11; Zech 9:9)

    Matthew's theological concern is to see the prophecy fulfilled literally by Jesus. This accounts for his curious suggestion that Jesus rode on donkey and foal: "they brought the donkey and the colt…and he sat on them" (v. 7). He had read Zechariah 9:9 as referring to two animals, whereas it is an instance of Hebraic parallelism. Matthew makes explicit what was implicit in Mark 11:1–11—Jesus' manner of entrance as a king: "humble and mounted on a donkey," fulfilled the prophecy in Zechariah 9:9.

11. 26:56: *But all this has taken place, so that the scriptures of the prophets might be fulfilled.*

    Matthew views the whole of the Old Testament as prophetic. The passion is about to begin. He places it under the rubric of fulfillment of prophecy. See 26:54: "But how then would the scriptures be fulfilled, which say it must happen in this way?" To be noted also is the text: "According to the definite plan and foreknowledge of God" (Acts 2:3).

12. 27:9–10: *Then was fulfilled what was spoken through the prophet Jeremiah, "and they took the thirty pieces of silver, the price of the one on whom a price had been set, on whom some of the people of Israel had a price, and they gave them for the potter's field, as the Lord commanded me."* (cf. Zech 11:13)

The quotation is not from Jeremiah but is loosely based on that of Zechariah 11:13. Faced with the enigma of Judas' betrayal of Jesus, Matthew utilizes again his concept of the fulfillment of Scripture. The traditional "thirty pieces of silver" (Matt 26:15) originates from Zechariah 11:12–13, which alludes to Exodus 21:32. In Zechariah, it is the paltry price paid to a rejected shepherd. Jesus is "handed over" to death by the salvific will of the Father, while Judas "betrays" (hands over) Jesus for the sake of money.

When we look at these reflection quotations together, what do we find? In the five Infancy Narrative quotations we learn that the virginally conceived Son of God is God-with-us; that, as son of David he was, fittingly, born in Bethlehem; that, in being called out of Egypt, he reenacted the Exodus of his people; that he suffered the Exile of his people, and that as the Nazorean—the man from Nazareth—he undertook his saving work. He began his mission by moving to Galilee and assuming the mantle of the Baptist. His journey to the ultimate passion involved his immersion in the pain and suffering of humankind. His path was one of humility and meekness, mirroring the pattern of the Almighty God, who displayed his omnipotence in the weakness of the Cross. The contemporary authorities did not grasp his paradoxical message; he spoke clearly to his disciples. His messianic entry into the city of the Messiah was marked by that meekness of his mission. It involved acceptance of betrayal. The betrayal and arrest of Jesus spotlight our human involvement in God's plan for us. There is God's mercy and there is human responsibility. Happily, they are not parallel: Human responsibility is fragile; God's mercy is divine. We commend Judas to God, not to humankind (see Matt 27:3–10; Acts 1:18–19).

Paradox

The Jesus of Matthew is a Jesus who cares—mirroring a God who cares. Ultimately, he is Emmanuel, God-with-us (1:23). Yet, in the Gospel, we also find a disturbing portrayal of God. For instance, in a codicil to the Lord's Prayer, we are warned that "if you do not forgive others, neither will your Father forgive your trespasses" (6:15). Judgment is severe: "I tell you, on the day of judgment you will have to give an account for every careless word you utter; for by your words will you be justified, and by your words will you be condemned" (12:36–37). The fate of any who lead simple Christians astray by callously shaking their faith is dire: "thrown into the eternal fire...thrown into the hell of fire" (18:8–9). More prominently, there are eight parables with vivid descriptions of violent consequences for those who do evil. Four of these are proper to Matthew: 13:36–43; 13:49–50; 18:23–35; 25:31–46. The others are: 21:33–46;

22:1–14; 24:45–51; 25:13–30. We look separately at them now.

1. 13:33–46. Explanation of the parable of the Weeds (13:24–30)

   The Son of Man is the sower. The good seed are the children of the kingdom; the weeds, children of the evil one. The sower of weeds is the devil. At the end of the age, angels, commissioned by the Son of Man, will gather all evildoers "and throw them into the furnace of fire, where there will be weeping and gnashing of teeth" (v. 42)—"Weeping and gnashing of teeth" is a favorite Matthean phrase, occurring no less than six times: 8:12; 13:42, 50; 22:13; 24:51; 25:30.

2. 13:47–50. The Net

   Fish, from a laden net, are sorted into good and bad. The lesson: "So it will be at the end of the age. The angels will come out and separate the evil from the righteous and throw them into the furnace of fire, where there will be weeping and gnashing of teeth" (vv. 49–50).

3. 18:28–35. The Unforgiving Servant

   A servant, owing a debt impossible of repayment, meets gracious cancellation of the debt. He will not show mercy to a fellow servant who owes a paltry sum. The king reacts harshly: "In anger his lord handed him over to be tortured until he should repay his entire debt" (v. 35). The lesson of this transparent allegory (God and sinner), is emphasized: "So my heavenly Father will also do to every one of you, if you do not forgive your brother or sister from your heart" (v. 35).

4. 21:33–46. The Wicked Tenants

Here we have another obvious allegory. Israel had rejected the prophets. The Son would be killed. His hearers answer the question of Jesus: What will the vineyard owner do to those tenants? "He will put those wretches to a miserable death, and lease out the vineyard to other tenants who will give him the produce at the harvest time" (v. 41).

5. 22:1–14. The Wedding Banquet

Guests invited to a wedding not only spurned the invitation but maltreated and even killed some of the messengers. An enraged king "sent his troops, destroyed those murderers and burned their city" (v. 8). In Matthew's addition (vv. 11–14) to the original parable (vv. 1–10) the king gave orders to his servants to expel an improperly attired guest: "Bind him hand and foot, and throw him into the outer darkness, where there will be weeping and gnashing of teeth" (v. 13).

6. 24:45–51. The Slave: Faithful or Unfaithful

A slave placed in charge of his household by a master embarking on a journey proved unfaithful.

The master, on his return, "will cut him to pieces and put him with the hypocrites, where there will be weeping and gnashing of teeth" (v. 51).

7. 25:14–30. The Talents

   Here the emphasis is on the slave who made no profit from the single talent he had received. His excuse: he knew his master to be "a harsh man, reaping where he did not sow" and "he was afraid" (vv. 24–25). The master accounts him "wicked and lazy" (v. 26) and gives order: "As for this worthless slave, throw him into the outer darkness, where there will be weeping and gnashing of teeth" (v. 30).

8. 25:31–45. Judgment on the Nations

   The King separates people on the basis of their caring or not caring for the poor, the needy, the suffering, and the marginalized. Those on the left are declared "accursed" and hear the sentence: "Depart from me into the eternal fire prepared for the devil and his angels" (v. 41). And the result: "Those [the accursed] will go away into eternal punishment, but the righteous into eternal life" (v. 46).

Barbara Reid observes that the punishment meted out to evildoers in these eight parables, where evildoers are thrown into a fiery furnace, crushed, destroyed, put to a miserable death, and cast into the outer darkness where there is weeping and gnashing of teeth, presents a vastly different image from the boundless ever-gracious God described in the Sermon on the Mount (5:44–48). Believers are faced with a serious dilemma: Which God is with us? In which one do we place our trust? Which one should we emulate?[3]

Here is a reasonable question indeed. The fact that Matthew is such a Jewish-Christian gospel may point to a solution. The Old Testament offers a key. We look to the "wrath" of God, which is a prominent feature in the prophets.

Wrath

The prophets of Israel proposed no theory of God, did not seek to expound the nature of God. They offered instead God's understanding of and concern for humanity. In particular, they offered an insight into the *pathos* of God—the Greek term refers to experience, to being intrinsically affected by events or persons. Pathos is not an attribute of God; rather it expresses God's loving care for creation. The basic feature of pathos is divine attentiveness and concern; the divine attention to humanity. Indeed, it is through his pathos, his relationship to Israel and to humanity, that we can know God at all. We can think of God only insofar as God thinks of us. God thinks of us always with concern. But, there is also the pathos of wrath.

It is undeniable that Scripture does speak of the "wrath" of God. God's "anger" is an aspect of divine pathos; it is a response to human sin. The biblical term *anger* denotes what we call righteous indignation. It is impatience with evil. Psalm

7:11 states that "God is a righteous judge, and a God who has indignation every day." In the Bible, a judge is not merely a person competent to consider a case and pronounce sentence, but one who is pained and distressed by injustice.

It is because God cares for humanity that his anger may be kindled against humans. Anger and mercy are not opposites but correlatives. Thus Habbakkuk prays: "In wrath remember mercy" (3:2). It is inconceivable that God's love should ever cease.[4]

The pathos of anger is never regarded as an attribute of God but as a response of God. In its origin and duration, it is clearly distinguished from mercy. This is beautifully expressed in Isaiah 54:7–8:

For a brief moment I abandoned you,
but with great compassion I will gather you.
In overflowing wrath for a moment
I hid my face from you,
but with everlasting love I will have compassion on you,
says the Lord, your Redeemer.

Note the radical imbalance between "overflowing wrath" and "everlasting love." Compassion flows from the love of a Redeemer; "wrath" is the grieving of a spurned Parent.

There is a biblical belief in divine grace, divine compassion. There is no belief in abiding and consuming divine anger. What is often proclaimed of love, for instance the refrain of Psalm 136: "for his steadfast love endures forever," is never said about anger. The normal and original pathos is love and mercy. It is only in the certainty that God's mercy is greater than his justice that the prophet could pray: "Although our iniquities testify against us, act, O Lord, for your name's sake" (Jer 14:7).

Paradox of Mercy

When one looks closely at the text of the prophetic books, one observes a striking and consistent factor. Not alone in the juxtaposition of oracles (prophetic pronouncements) but, regularly, within an oracle, we find an abrupt change of mood. There is warning and threat, often extensive, to a stubborn and unfaithful people, and then suddenly comes word of salvation. There is no logic to it, but therein lie the beauty and the comfort. There is no logic because salvation is sheer grace.

Jeremiah (chapters 29–33) speaks of hope after the disaster that was the destruction of Jerusalem and the Babylonian exile, and where we meet the sharp contrast:

For thus says the Lord:
Your hurt is incurable,
    your wound is grievous.
There is no one to uphold your cause,
    no medicine for your wound,
    no healing for you…
Because your guilt is great,
    because your sins are so numerous…
    I have done these things to you. (30:12–15)

The ring of finality seems to exclude all hope. Then, abruptly, is the assurance:

I will restore health to you
and your wounds I will heal,
says the Lord. (30:17)

Incurable hurt; no healing available—I will restore health, I will heal! God can do; God will do, what is humanly impossible. He acts in virtue of his infinite love.

The remarkable fluctuation we have observed in the prophets can be documented over and over. It is not a rarity; it is the norm. And the flow is always in the same direction: threat is followed by words of hope and salvation. The pattern surely means that God's final word is mercy and forgiveness. And this feature is found not only in the prophets. The God of the Bible, the Father of our Lord Jesus Christ, is the foolish God. (See 1 Cor 1:18–25).[5]

Matthew stands in this tradition. His words of threat are in line with the stern words of the prophets. They mean that God is serious in his demands. He knows what he wants his children to be. As loving Parent, he speaks not only invitation but warning. He remains always the gracious Parent of infinite love, and throughout the Gospel of Matthew, Jesus, who is God-with-us, does present this Father—his Father, and ours.

NOTES

1. Daniel J. Harrington, "Matthew as a Jewish Book," *Priests & People* 7 (1993): 242.

2. John P. Meier, *Matthew* (Wilmington, DE: Michael Glazier, 1980), 132–33.

3. Barbara, E. Reid, "Which God is With Us?," *Interpretation* 64, no. 4, (October 2010): 380–89 at 385.

4. Abraham Heschel, *The Prophets* (New York: Harper & Row, 2001), 364.

5. Wilfrid J. Harrington, *The Loving God* (Dublin: The Columba Press, 2012), 31–40; *Hold On to Hope. The Foolishness of God* (Dublin: Dominican Publications, 1998), 13–53.

CHAPTER 2

BIRTH OF THE CHRIST

Each of the evangelists tells his readers, at the outset, who this Jesus is: the source and center of the Good News they proclaim. Mark does it with commendable succinctness: "The beginning of the good news of Jesus Christ, the Son of God" (1:1). John does it in his distinctive manner: "In the beginning was the Word...And the Word became flesh and dwelt among us" (1:1, 14). Matthew and Luke do it in their Infancy Narratives (Matt 1—2; Luke 1—2). While our concern is with Matthew's focus on Jesus as Teacher, the evangelist is clearly conscious of him as one far more profound, which he reveals in his Infancy Narrative. The Teacher, in his sermons, will speak with the authority of "the Messiah, the son of David" who is Emmanuel, God-with-us (1:1, 23).

PROLOGUE: BIRTH OF THE MESSIAH (1—2)

She will bear a son, and you are to name him Jesus, for he will save his people from their sins.

Matthew 1:21

The Genealogy of Jesus the Messiah 1:1–17

The Old Testament, especially Genesis and 1 Chronicles, makes skillful use of genealogies. Similarly, Matthew finds his genealogy to be an effective way of establishing the identity of Jesus. He traces Jesus' ancestry back to David and Abraham: "An account of the genealogy of Jesus the Messiah, the son of David, the son of Abraham" (1:1). He shows that the one whom Christians proclaim to be "Messiah" (Christ) can be correctly named "Son of David." No doubt he turned to the Scriptures, finding in 1 Chronicles 2:1–5 and Ruth 4:18–22 his sources for 1:2–6a and in 1 and 2 Kings the list of kings given in 1:6b–11. First Chronicles and a popular genealogy of the Davidic Messiah provided the names in 1:12–16 to which Matthew added Joseph, Mary, and Jesus.

Matthew's pattern of three sets of fourteen generations is patently artificial; to get his "fourteen generations" from David to the Exile, he passed over in silence some of the kings of Judah. He appears to have been influenced by current apocalyptic thought, which cast world history in periods of seven, in other words "weeks" of years. For Israel's history, Matthew counts "two 'weeks' of generations (2 x 7 = 14 generations), from Israel's beginnings in Abraham to its high point in King David, two more weeks from its high point to its low point in the disaster of the Babylonian exile, and two further weeks during its ascent to its goal, Jesus the Messiah. Jesus Christ thus begins the seventh period, the period of perfection and fulfillment (see Daniel's seventy weeks of years in Dan 9). Hence, Matthew uses an apocalyptic convention to proclaim that God has secretly ordered the economy of salvation so that all of Israel's history moves smoothly towards the Messiah."[1]

One must note that this Jesus is not only son of David—he is also "the son of Abraham." As such he is the fulfillment of the promise that through Abraham "all the nations of the earth" would be blessed (Gen 12:3; 22; 18). Significantly, the Gospel closes with the commission to "make disciples of all nations" (Matt 28:19). With his designation of Jesus as "the son of David, the son of Abraham," Matthew is declaring the Messiah to be the Savior (1:21) of Jew and Gentile.

When one reads Matthew's list, we are, to some extent, faced with names. However, we can put faces on a goodly number of the names, not all of which are prepossessing. Jesus' ancestry is not altogether a saintly line; it is, in generous measure, disreputable. True, it begins on a high note, with Abraham, the man of faith, followed by a weak Isaac, and a rascally Jacob. It is comforting to stress this aspect of the genealogy. One might suggest that Matthew is making the same point as the author of Hebrews: the sinless Jesus is "like his brothers and sisters in every respect" (Heb 2:17). He had no control over his ancestry. There is, too, the comforting assurance that God "can write straight on crooked lines," that inadequate humans cannot thwart his purpose. They may indeed serve his purpose.

The Women

A fascinating feature of Matthew's genealogy is the prominence of women. One would have expected Mary, of course, but not the others: Tamar, Rahab, Ruth, Bathsheba. Their presence is due to the fact that they are "holy irregularities": there is something not quite regular in the relationship of each with her spouse. Tamar (Gen 38) is an obvious example. She had been married to Er, son of Judah, who died without issue. According to levirate law (Deut 25:5–6), it was the duty of the next son, Onan, to marry the widow; the first son of that union would be regarded as son of the deceased, so guaranteeing the only immortality he might have.[2]

Tamar had been hard done by her father-in-law, who would deprive her of her legal right. Her claim was not selfish: she was upholding the cause of her dead husband. She took the law into her own hands. In the event, Judah has to admit: "She is more righteous than I" (Gen 38:26). To see in Tamar's conduct an instance of the end justifying the means is an obvious temptation and a glaring instance of missing the point of the biblical story. In context, it is obvious that her conduct was admirable: she was a woman of her day and age. She had done no more than the exploited widow of Jesus' parable: she had, in the face of male callousness, taken a womanly way to get her way (see Luke 18:2–5). A message is that the little ones of this world, the marginalized, have a God-given right to vindicate their rights. Is this not after all the message of the *Magnificat*?

Rahab and Ruth are less easy to assess. In the genealogy, Rahab appears as wife of Salmon and mother of Boaz. She is certainly the Rahab of Joshua 2—the prostitute, who had sheltered Joshua's spies. A snag is that Boaz comes nearly two centuries later than the age of Joshua; a marriage of Rahab and Salmon is unlikely, to put it mildly! To overcome this problem, biblical writers would look to the meaning of the story rather than our concern of whether it is true or not. In this sense, Rahab was a woman who had read the writing on the wall. Jericho was doomed; she cut her losses and threw in her lot with the eventual conquerors. Not very noble, perhaps, but surely very human.

Ruth, a Moabitess, having lost her Israelite husband, elected to remain with her mother-in-law, Naomi. The shrewd older woman was able to engineer a marriage for Ruth with Boaz, kinsman of her late husband. There is more than a suggestion that he was cleverly manipulated by the women. But all turned out well. Ruth became the great-grandmother of David. Ruth is a touching human story. As in the case of Tamar, there is concern for the right of a dead husband. There is, in Naomi and Ruth, an edifying bond of love between mother-in-law and daughter-in-law. Furthermore, there is the charming touch: two admirable women, who gently manipulate an admirable man.

Bathsheba, "the wife of Uriah," is different (2 Sam 11). It is clear that she was not notably upset at having caught the attention of King David. And there is no evidence of overwhelming grief at the death of her husband. Indeed, her major role in winning the throne for her son, Solomon, and his obvious acknowledgment of her part (1 Kgs 1—2), makes clear that she was an ambitious woman, and probably the least attractive of the four, who, each in her own manner, were foils to Mary and her "holy irregularity"—virginal conception. More importantly, these women played a significant role in God's plan; observe the initiative of Rahab and Ruth. All four of them continued the lineage of the Messiah, in which Matthew clearly sees the hand of God.

We can ask ourselves if we have anything like Tamar's passion for justice. Rahab might alert us to a temptation to cut our losses. True, she had ended up on the winning side—but could she really live with herself? The love of the older and the younger women, Naomi and Ruth, of different nationalities, is surely a headline. There is also the message that romance, along with a dash of female charm, are precious human values. We should be grateful that we have the gift of the Song of Songs, that celebration of sexual love. Finally, there is the less savory but no less human side. The love affair of David and Bathsheba led to the callous murder of an innocent Uriah. We are joyously reminded that human love, when it is truly such, is God's wonderful gift to humankind. We are also painfully reminded that we humans can pervert love. The four women are, in diverse ways, a radical challenge to us. They are a challenge to what can be best and what might be worst in our humanness.

Matthew's genealogy informs the reader that Jesus is "son of David" and "son of Abraham." Matthew leaves the "son of Abraham" motif and its Gentile connotation until the story of the Magi (2:1–12) and concentrates first on the son of David. What emerges is that Jesus is of the Messianic line. What we have been at pains to show is that he is of *this* line. Here is documentation to back up the assertion in Hebrews that he is like us in all things. Jesus of Nazareth is of the human family of David. Jesus the Savior is of the human race. There is our comfort and our hope.

The Infancy Narrative 1:18—2:23

The Infancy Narratives of Matthew and Luke have had a notable influence on Christian tradition and have put a profound mark on Christian art. The long Christian appreciation of them has not been misplaced. We had sensed that there is something special here—that these texts say more than they appear to say. In fact, we have happily come to realize that both infancy narratives, which are wholly independent of each other, are, first and foremost, Christological statements. It is in this sense that we can grasp their true meaning.[3]

Matthew 1—2

Matthew and Luke share a twofold tradition: Jesus' home was Nazareth; Jesus was descendent of David and, as such, appropriately born in Bethlehem. Reconciliation of these traditions has influenced the shape of their narratives. For Matthew, Jesus' birth in Bethlehem offered no problem; in his view, Bethlehem was home of Joseph and Mary. He has to move Jesus from Bethlehem to Nazareth. For Luke, on the other hand, the home of Joseph and Mary was Nazareth. He has to arrange to have Jesus born in Bethlehem. This contrived reconciliation, by each evangelist, of the dominant Nazareth tradition (throughout the Gospels Jesus is regarded as a Nazarene) with the Bethlehem tradition, would suggest that birth at Bethlehem is to be taken as a *theologoumenon* (a theological affirmation related as an historical event)—in this case an affirmation of the Davidic descent of Jesus. In any event, whether his place of birth was Bethlehem or Nazareth, what matters is that Jesus of Nazareth was wholly one of us.

In building his infancy narrative, Matthew has made use of two main blocks of material: a cycle of angelic dream appearances, and the Magi story, both of which have been thoroughly edited by Matthew.

The Cycle of Angelic Dream Appearances

A. 1:20–25; B. 2:13–15; C. 2:19–22

1. An angel of the Lord appeared to Joseph in a *dream* (1:20; 2:13; 2:20).
2. The angel gave a *command* (1:20; 2:13; 2:20).
3. The angel offered a *reason* for the command (1:20–21; 2:13; 2:20).
4. Joseph rose and *fulfilled* the command (1:24–25; 2:14–15a; 2:21).

It is evident that Joseph wears the cloak of the famous patriarch Joseph (Gen 37—50), especially in his being a man of dreams and in his going down to Egypt.

As noted earlier, a feature of Matthew's Gospel is his use of reflection citations (Old Testament quotations) that sit loosely in their context. They are notably frequent in his infancy narrative: 1:22–23; 2:5–6; 2:15; 2:17–18; 2:23. Matthew has recognized the applicability of certain Old Testament texts to particular incidents in Jesus' career. He introduced them because they fit his theology of the oneness of God's plan and because they help to bring out, for his Christian readers, who and what Jesus is. Thus, the five infancy narrative citations tell us that the virginally conceived Jesus is God-with-us; that, as son of David, he was born in Bethlehem; that, in being called out of Egypt, he reenacted the Exodus of his people; that he suffered the Exile of his people, and that as the Nazorean, he began his saving work.

The Birth of Jesus 1:18–25

Joseph and Mary were betrothed. In Jewish society, betrothal is something far more serious than our marriage engagement. Betrothal is really a marriage contract except that the partners have not begun to live together. Joseph discovered that his betrothed was pregnant—"of the Holy Spirit" is Matthew's nod to the reader. Joseph was not aware of that factor and was in a quandary. He was a "righteous" man, that is, Law-observant. He assumed that Mary had been unfaithful. The death penalty for adultery (Deut 22:23–27) was not then, if ever it had been, in force; divorce was the solution, and was the course on which Joseph had decided on—except that he wanted to divorce her "quietly." It is not clear how he could have hoped to achieve this, and divorce would certainly not have helped Mary at all. She would have been left on her own to bear her baby; an unmarried mother in a thoroughly disapproving society. The "righteous" man, Joseph, was confused. He desperately wanted to do the "decent" thing, but his "solution" was no solution at all.

Happily for him, and for Mary, God took a hand. All was made clear in a dream. Mary was not an unfaithful bride, but a wholly privileged instrument of God. Her child, of divine parenthood, would be the Savior; the one who "will save his people from their sins." It is here that Matthew throws in his reflection citation. He looked to Isaiah 7:14 (in the Greek) and found there a word of promise: "the young woman is with child and shall bear a son." That son will be Emmanuel, God-with-us. Cleverly, Matthew has anticipated the close of his gospel: "Remember, I am with you always" (28:20). In that unique child of Mary, a first-century Palestinian Jew, we meet our God. Paul had put it in his inimitable fashion: "In Christ God was reconciling the world to himself" (2 Cor 5:19).

The Magi Story 2:1–12

In this narrative, Matthew inserts into the infancy event the reactions that historically greeted the proclamation of the risen Lord: some believed and paid homage; others rejected the message and the preachers. In other words, the Christological revelation was followed by proclamation and by the twofold reaction of acceptance/homage and rejection/persecution. But this had been prepared for in the ministry of Jesus. The same pattern is presented in the infancy narrative.

The negative reaction of Herod and his advisors—the chief priests and scribes—turns the infancy narrative into a veritable gospel, which must have suffering and rejection as well as success.

As it stands, 2:1–12 is a self-contained story, with no mention of Joseph. There seems little point in looking for the homeland of the Magi, whom Matthew regards seemingly as astrologers of some sort. Nor is there any point in looking to a comet, a supernova, or a planetary conjunction to account for "his star" (1:2). A star that rises, goes before, and comes to rest over a place is not a natural phenomenon but a miraculous (more precisely, a symbolic) star. More to the point is that, for Matthew, the Magi represent the Gentiles, notably alerted not by an angel (as Luke's Jewish shepherds) but by a star. The liturgical tradition of the feast of Epiphany has caught Matthew's intent. The Magi's role as prefiguring the acceptance of Gentiles into the Christian community points toward the universal character of the gospel. Jesus is functioning as son of Abraham.

The Balaam narrative of Numbers 22—24, embroidered with Jewish tradition and skillfully used by Matthew, appears to have been the inspiration of the Magi story. Balaam, a seer, was summoned by Balak "from the east" to curse Israel. Significantly, the Alexandrian Jewish philosopher Philo calls him a *magos.* Herod tried to use the magi for his own ends as Balak had tried to get a *magos* to destroy his enemy, only to have him bless his enemy. Herod tried to manipulate the magi: they ended up worshiping the "enemy" he had sought to destroy. In his oracle, Balaam had declared: "A star shall rise from Jacob, and a man shall stand forth from Israel" [Greek] (Num 24:17). The oracle refers to David, and here, credibly, is "his star" (Matt 2:2).

Matthew has the Magi joyfully follow the guiding star to the house where they found child and mother—the house being the Bethlehem home of Joseph and Mary. Fittingly, they had brought gifts for the king: gifts of gold (Ps 72:10–15), frankincense (Isa 60:6) and myrrh (like frankincense, an aromatic gum), suggestive of *three* magi (Matthew does not specify), and the gifts themselves were given symbolic meanings.

Herod, the Chief Priests, and Scribes

Herod the Great was, by grace of Rome, king of Judea 37 BC to AD 4. He was an able and energetic ruler, at least in Roman eyes. In the domestic sphere, his reign was deeply troubled. Of a suspicious nature (in 29 BC he had his favorite wife, Mariamne, executed for alleged adultery), he was jealous of his power and reacted violently to any suspected threat. In 28 BC, his mother-in-law was put to death on a charge of plotting against him. In 27 BC, Alexander and Rufus, his sons by Mariamne, were killed, and a few days before his own death, the king had his son, Antipater, executed. This Herod is recognizable in the Herod of Matthew.

The evangelist has introduced "all the chief priests and scribes of the people" as advisers of the sinister Herod (2:3–5). It might appear that they do no more than answer a theological question. Matthew certainly implies something else. In the first place, they, too, must have been "troubled" by the Magi's word of the birth of the Messiah. They could not have been deceived by Herod's feigned piety. Knowing that he was paranoid on the subject of any threat to his throne, they should have realized that he would not look kindly upon an infant "king of the Jews." By disclosing to him the birthplace of the Messiah, they became, effectively, collaborators in his evil intent. In fact, it is they, not Herod, who will eventually bring about the death of the "king of the Jews." It is "the chief priests and elders of the people" who will plot to arrest and kill Jesus (26:3–5, 47; 27:1–2, 12, 20); "the scribes" are mentioned in 26:57 and 27:41. They are those who have their own understanding of religion; they are those who jealously guard their status and privilege (cf. John 11:48). They cannot be open to the word of this birth, just as they will not be open to the message of Jesus and will want to get rid of him. He was a threat to Herod and to them: to the throne of the former, and to the religious empire of the latter.

Flight and Return 2:13–23

The next two episodes are colored by the story of Moses in Egypt as elaborated in Jewish tradition, and also echo the Exodus motif. The basic storyline in 2:13–15 concerns the rescue of a child savior from the machinations of the wicked king by flight into Egypt. Jewish tradition, as we find it, for example, in Flavius Josephus, had it that the Pharaoh of the Exodus had been forewarned by one of his "sacred scribes" of the birth of a Hebrew who would constitute a threat to the Egyptian kingdom. Pharaoh and the whole of Egypt were filled with dread (see Matt 2:3). Pharaoh's plan was frustrated by a warning communicated in a dream to Moses' father. The parallels between the Jewish legend and the pre-Matthean infancy narrative are manifest. With the background of Exodus 1—2, Jesus emerges as a Moses-figure. The Hosea quotation—"Out of Egypt have I called my son"—refers to the exodus of Israel from Egypt. Matthew sees that Jesus relives the history of his people, not only in the Exile, but in the previous going down into Egypt.

The storyline in 2:16–18, involving the massacre of the male children in Bethlehem, echoes Pharaoh's decree against the male children of the Hebrews. Matthew, with his formula citation of Jeremiah 31:15, works in another theme: that of the Babylonian Exile. Again, Jesus is associated with a tragic event of his people. The names in the three quotations: Bethlehem (the city of David), Egypt (the land of the Exodus), and Ramah (the mourning place of the Exile) are theologically suggestive. The final episode (2:19–23) also gives us three significant names: Israel, Galilee, and Nazareth. The "quotation" here is not really such: Matthew is playing on the name Nazareth. Quite likely, he is thinking of the *neser*, "branch" of Isa 11:1 and of *nazir*, "one consecrated to God." At any rate, he knows that this son of David, Son of God, is none other than Jesus, the Nazorean.

NOTES

1. John P. Meier, *Matthew* (Wilmington, DE: Michael Glazier, 1980), 3–4.

2. One should note that not until the second century BC was there, in Israel, any real notion of an afterlife. Life ended in the gloom of Sheol—in effect, the grave.

3. I acknowledge my indebtedness to the scholarship of Raymond E. Brown, *The Birth of the Messiah, New Updated Edition* (New York: Doubleday, 1993).

CHAPTER 3

SERMON ON THE MOUNT

The Sermon on the Mount is the first of Matthew's five discourses. The setting (5:1) and the conclusion (7:28–29) indicate that, in his plan, the Sermon was addressed to all Israel gathered to hear Jesus. The basic theme is that Jesus came not to abolish the Law and the Prophets (the Old Testament) but to fulfill them (5:17). Matthew had Jews in mind. More immediately, he has Jesus present what Christians must accept as his authoritative interpretation of Torah. For Matthew, this Sermon is the charter of Christian faith and practice.

The Outline of the Sermon:

Introduction 5:1–20
The Antitheses 5:21–48
Three Acts of Piety 6:1–18
Other Teachings 6:19—7:12
Warnings 7:13–29

INTRODUCTION

The Beatitudes (5:1–12)

The Gospels of Matthew and Luke present two notably different versions of the beatitudes: Matthew 5:3–12 and Luke 6:20–23. Matthew has nine beatitudes while Luke has only four, but with four corresponding "woes" (6:24–26). Both versions have grown from an original core originating from Jesus, the additions and adaptations being due to the evangelists. The beatitudes of Jesus are three:

- Blessed are the poor, for the kingdom of heaven is theirs.
- Blessed are those who hunger, for they will be filled.
- Blessed are the afflicted, for they will be comforted.

These beatitudes do not refer to three separate categories but to three aspects of the same distressful situation. What merit, one may ask, is there in being poor, hungry, afflicted? There is none. The "blessedness" of the poor is in their very need, their distress. God is their champion, as he showed himself to be in Jesus.

Luke has three beatitudes, plus a fourth: the blessedness of those who suffer persecution for the sake of Christ. And he, like Jesus, looks to the really poor and afflicted. Matthew's longer version contains only three new beatitudes: the merciful, the pure in heart, and the peacemakers. We get a total of nine only because those of the poor/meek and the last two (the persecuted) are duplicates. But there are distinctive features in Matthew's beatitudes. The expression "pure in spirit" points to a transformation of the idea of "the poor." In current usage, the designation "poor in spirit" applies to one who is detached from worldly goods, who is interiorly free in regard to money. While it is possible for an economically rich person to be "poor in spirit," the expression is related frequently to the possession of wealth. This is because we take "poor" in a specific economic sense, which may not be the biblical meaning. We now know from the Jewish texts of Qumran that "poor" is equivalent to "humility": the poor in spirit are the humble. The parallel beatitude of "the meek" confirms this meaning. These beatitudes in Matthew are no longer addressed to those who lack the necessities of life (as for Jesus and Luke) but to those characterized by their meekness, their patience, their humility. They are *anawim*, with Jesus himself as the ultimate "poor man" (1:29). It is evident that "blessed are those who hunger and thirst for righteousness" is very different from Luke's blessedness of the "poor" and the "hungry." For Matthew, Christianity has broadened and deepened the meaning of the term "righteousness" (cf. 5:20).

Among the new beatitudes, we look first at "blessed are the pure in heart for they shall see God" (5:8). The qualification "in heart," like "in spirit," points to an interior disposition. What we would call "purity of intention" is in question, demanding perfect correspondence between intention and action. The beatitudes of the merciful and the peacemakers are concerned with action, the conduct of a Christian towards a neighbor who stands in need. The best illustration of "merciful" occurs in Matthew's description of the last judgment: "I was hungry and you gave me food..." (25:35–40). The role of "peacemakers" represents a good work, and is highly prized in Judaism. It was observed that, among those who need help, the most in need are often an estranged husband and wife, or friends who have fallen out. To seek to reconcile and to restore them to peace is one of the kindest services one can render to the neighbor.

Where Luke applies the beatitudes to Christians as a suffering minority, Matthew introduces a distinction; he reserves the promise of blessedness in the beatitudes to Christians who truly live the gospel ideal. He has related the beatitudes in light of his pastoral preoccupation and expands on them. He takes care to remind Christians that the promises of salvation are conditional (5:20). We will not be admitted to the Kingdom unless, after the example of the Master, we have shown ourselves to be meek and humble; unless we have given proof of loyalty and righteousness; unless we have carried out what God has asked of us; and in particular, unless we have served our brothers and sisters in their need.

In 5:13–16 the link with the beatitudes to persecution immediately preceding them is intentional: though Christians are persecuted by the world, they are, nonetheless, the world's salvation. The Christian disciple is "salt of the earth." The true disciple of Jesus can never rest content with one's state of blessedness in the sight of God. One's own faith and way of life have an apostolic dimension. One must display one's "good deeds" before the world. If disciples lose their sense of purpose and do not witness to the world, they will become as useless as unrefined Dead Sea salt, which could lose its saltiness. They could end up by being rejected (5:13).

If Jesus is "the light of the world" (John 8:12), his disciples are meant to enlighten. They should be as conspicuous by their manner of life as a village on a Galilean hillside. The Christian is a lamp designed to give light; one betrays one's calling if one lives only for oneself. Christians ought to bear witness before fellow Christians and before unbelievers. This is their calling. Those who are brought to Christ by their witness will give the glory to the heavenly Father (5:13–16).

The Principle (5:17–20)

"Do not think that I have come to abolish the law or the prophets; I have come not to abolish but to fulfill" (5:17). The opening passage (5:17–20) sets the tone in relating the Mosaic Law to Jesus. Jesus has not come to reject "the law and the prophets." His mission is one of prophetic fulfillment. Nor did he come to *obey* the Law. He transcends it, so that he, not the Law, becomes the norm for the Christian. This is borne out by verse 18: "until all is accomplished" refers to the event of the death-resurrection of Jesus. Post-Easter Christians will live by the "law" of Jesus (cf. 7:24). Nevertheless, the Christian teacher will be faithful to the Law, as reinterpreted by Jesus (v.19). Christians are not to become better "Pharisees" and turn into legalists. Christianity is meant to have broadened and deepened the meaning of the term "righteousness"; the doing of God's will, according to the teaching of Jesus.

THE ANTITHESES (5:21–48)

The principle outlined in verses 17–20 is applied in the "antitheses" (5:21–48). Six times, with a similar formula each time, the law is quoted ("you have heard that it was said") to be followed by an "antithetical" word of Jesus that modifies it ("but I say to you"). In the cases of murder, adultery, and love, Jesus radicalized the Law by extension and internalization; in the cases of divorce, oaths, and retaliation, he abrogated the letter of the Law.

The first antithesis (vv. 21–26) declares that anger is as grave a crime as murder. Jesus interprets the fifth commandment so that it embraces all those feelings and emotions of which murder is the outcome. He moves on to strong recommendation of brotherly/sisterly reconciliation and warns that an unforgiving spirit will come between us and the God we would worship. In the second antithesis (vv. 27–30), we are warned that adultery, too, is born in the heart. The sixth commandment, as reinterpreted by Jesus, reaches to all thoughts and desires that lead to sexual sin. One must have firmly in mind that Jesus, as a Jew, had a positive and healthy approach to human sexuality. There is no trace, in his teaching, of the neurosis that was to mark, so sadly, a prevalent strain in Christian attitudes to sexuality.

In the third antithesis (vv. 31–32), Jesus revokes the law's sanctioning of divorce (see Deut 24:1–4). Puzzling is the qualification "except on the ground of unchastity" (see Matt 19:9). It now seems reasonable to hold (evidence from the Qumran documents has helped) that by "unchastity" (*porneia*), Matthew means marriages within prohibited degrees of consanguinity and affinity: "incestuous" marriages. There is no question of divorce in such cases because there is no marriage to begin with. Jesus forbade divorce without qualification. The fourth antithesis (vv. 33–37) is a radical rejection of a respected institution of the Torah: oaths and vows. The Matthean Jesus categorically declares: "Do not swear *at all*!" There is no way of reconciling this absolute prohibition with later church practice (recall the obligation of the anti-modernistic oath). And, to this day, there is the demand of a seemingly modified oath—an oath of fidelity that is mandatory for one assuming ecclesiastical office—but one which, on closer reading, is more restrictive than the former. Surely, this should make us think.

Too often the law of *talion*, "an eye for an eye and a tooth for a tooth" is cited as an image of primitive savagery. On the contrary, it is an enlightened law designed to regulate and moderate retaliation—to "make the punishment fit the crime" (see Exod 21:4; Lev 24:20; Deut 19:21). Here again, Jesus revokes the letter of the Torah. Not "a tooth for a tooth," careful correspondence of injury and compensation, but radical repudiation of any retaliation: "Turn the other cheek also." G. B. Caird's illuminating comment opens up a wider perspective:

> When one man wrongs another, the other may retaliate, bear a grudge, or take his injury out on a third person. Whichever he does there are now two evils where before there was one, and a chain reaction is started, like the spreading of a contagion.

> Only if the victim absorbs the wrong and so puts it out of currency, can it be prevented from going any further.[1]

Jesus rules out all means, even legal action, of obtaining compensation.

Despite the formulation of verse 43, nowhere in the Law does it state that the Israelite should hate the enemy. We are faced with a popular modification of the love-command: the enemy of the just person or of God's people is an enemy of God. Besides, "neighbor" would have been restricted to fellow Jews and, consequently, there is no obligation to love the "non-neighbor." Jesus broadened the range of "neighbor" to apply to all without distinction of race (see Luke 10:29–37). He is not taking a sentimental or naïve view that all people are, in practice, brothers and sisters. He maintains the category of enemy. If he demands love of enemies it is because the Father loves those whom we would count as his enemies. Unless they can display this all-embracing love, Christians are no better than others; they have not really experienced the love of their Parent. Matthew speaks of perfection: "Be perfect, therefore, as your heavenly Father is perfect" (v. 48). Here, "perfection" means maturity, full development. Matthew has in mind generous single-hearted devotion to God and humankind. This is why to be "perfect" is the obligation of every Christian, or, at very least, our abiding challenge.

These demands, throughout the antitheses, are not intended as regulations for the conduct of daily life. But they are meant to be taken seriously. They are vivid and even startling illustrations of the manner in which the quality and directness of God's treatment of his children might be reproduced in human relationships. Jesus was wholly aware of how much he asked of human nature when he substituted "love your enemies" for "love your neighbor."

THREE ACTS OF PIETY (6:1–18)

Almsgiving, prayer, and fasting were traditional Jewish practices. In each case, it is a question of a private act of piety, admirable when performed simply by sincere people. "Hypocrites" can make an unholy show of these good ways. Like chapter 23, the passage 6:1–18 is an attack on the Jewish opponents of Matthew's community. In chapter 23 the "hypocrites" say but do not do; here what they do is for show. Public displays of private piety are not for Jesus' followers.

One can readily see that, originally, the passage was made up of the three units 6:2–4, 5–6, 16–18—the uniform construction of the units makes that clear. It is obvious that Matthew took advantage of the reference to prayer here to fill out the teaching of Jesus on the subject (6:7–15).

"And when you pray, you must not be like the hypocrites" (6:5). While the "hypocrites" are the Jewish opponents, they also represent a legalistic element within Matthew's community. "When you are praying"; it is assumed that Christians do pray. What is in question is how they ought to pray, or, in the first instance, how they ought *not* to pray. They must not make a spectacle of prayer. In verses 7–8 there is another negative precept, but this time in view of Gentile practice. Invocation of pagan deities was regularly a fulsome affair.

The gods' attention had to be attracted, hence a prelude of elaborate titles and adulatory attributes. There is no need for any of this when one turns, trustfully, to an Abba (cf. the Psalms). These negative rulings had cleared the way for the positive teaching of the Lord: "Pray then in this way" (6:9).

The Lord's Prayer (6:9–13)

Matthew (6:9–13) and Luke (11:2–4) provide two versions of the Lord's Prayer. The first and obvious difference is that Matthew's version is longer. More importantly, Matthew has preserved the original strongly eschatological flavor of the prayer, while Luke has adapted it to fit the modest pattern of day-to-day Christian living. Besides, the Matthean version is notably Jewish in tone, clearly congenial to Jewish Christians.

The first three petitions (vv. 9–10) really lead to the central one: "Your kingdom come." The disciples pray that God will show forth his saving will by bringing about his definitive Rule over humankind. The petition, "Give us this day our daily bread" (v. 11) should very likely read: "Give us today our bread for the coming day"; that is to say the bread of the banquet in the kingdom.

The plea for the forgiveness of all sins ("debts") also looks to the end, when sin will be no more. And, we pray not to be crushed by the great temptation, the end-time crisis, to escape, at last and forever, the designs of the Evil One. From first to last it is a prayer of faith and hope, a prayer that looks confidently beyond this world to the rule of the Father. The plea for forgiveness in verse 12 is underscored by the codicil of verses 14–15. The implication is that we are expected to forgive others before we plead for God's forgiveness of us (cf. Sir 28:1–5). Indeed (as the prayer stands) we make our forgiveness of others a condition of God's forgiveness of us. Matthew's commentary simply makes unmistakable the sense of the petition: "For if you forgive others their trespasses, your heavenly Father will also forgive you; but if you do not forgive others, neither will your Father forgive your trespasses" (6:14–15; cf. Matt 18:21–35). The obligation of forgiveness cannot be stressed more clearly for us—that God does not really temper his boundless mercy to our grudging forgiveness. What he expects of us is clear.

"When you fast" (6:16–17): the only fast enjoined in the Torah is on the Day of Atonement (cf. Lev 16; 31; 23:26–32). Pious Pharisees fasted each Monday and Thursday. This practice, as such, is not being criticized. Again, it is a matter of parading what should have been private observance. "Your Father who sees in secret will reward you" (vv. 4, 6, 17): God is the one who not only observes, but rewards good deeds done in secret.

OTHER TEACHINGS (6:19—7:12)

There is no obvious structure to the third part of the Sermon (6:19—7:12). Jesus cautions his disciples against worldly standards: the "treasures" of the world are tawdry and fragile. What he calls for is "purity of heart." A person's heart is where one's treasure is (6:21). There is a basic decision: one must choose to worship ("serve") the one true God, the heavenly Father, or the false god of worldly possessions. Jesus came to reveal the Father to men and women, to assure them that they are not alone. The Father loves them and cares for them. We are in constant danger of becoming immersed in the affairs of this world and of allowing them to ensnare us. Here Jesus calls on us to pass beyond a care for material things to a consideration of higher values. Humankind is made for God and only in God can we find rest (6:24).

The general theme of the passage 6:25–30 is expressed in a wealth of imagery and, in a style that is typically Matthean, with pairs of images. The wild flowers and grasses shape a particularly telling image of transience. After the rains in Palestine, there is a short period when the arid and rocky scrub soil is covered with delicate wild flowers. In a few weeks, they have withered to yellow, brittle stalks.

Jesus' words are meant to highlight the reality of God's care. God is not an impersonal force remote from this world. He is very much present, even when he may seem to be absent. Jesus is not condemning human industry or resourcefulness. We must plan for the morrow. The beauty of the lilies fades and birds die of hunger. We, too, will shrivel unless we use our God-given talents.

What Jesus calls on us to avoid is not the normal concern demanded by our human condition but the fretting that dehumanizes us, the worry that keeps us from lifting our gaze beyond material values and the cares of this world. The concluding proverb (v. 34) is not really as enigmatic as it sounds. Each day has its burden of problems; it does not help to add the morrow's problems to the load. The Christian will look not to a fleeting "tomorrow" but to the solid future of the kingdom. We will put our future in the hands of God and pray only for the modest needs of today.

A caution: We are not to be too ready to pass judgment on others. We are adept at spotting the faults of others. A touch of humor: if we could but see ourselves, many of us walking about with big planks sticking out of our eyes while we peer at a speck in our neighbor's eye! (7:1–5). As for prayer: ask...seek...knock!—even though your Father knows your need before you ask (see 6:8). Why ask then? God does not need our prayer. We need God; we need to acknowledge our dependence; we must seek and knock. The need is ours. Think of mother and child: a loving mother knows what is best for her child. The child may ask, may demand; but she will give only what is helpful. A firm "no" is often the most loving answer. We should never forget that "no" is quite as much an answer as "yes"—even to prayer!

WARNINGS (7:13–29)

The road to the kingdom is no four-lane highway—there is a narrow gate at the end of it. In passage 7:13–14 the motif of the two gates is joined with that of the two ways. Each way leads to a gate: to perdition or to eternal life. The motif of the "Two Ways" was traditional in the ancient world. In the Old Testament it is found most prominently in Deuteronomy 11:26–28; 30:15–20. There is a stark choice. It is Matthew's view that entrance to the kingdom is difficult; not many will get there. He reflects the pessimism of 4 Ezra: "I said before, and I say now, and will say it again: There are more who perish than those who will be saved, as a wave is greater than a drop of water" (9:15–16). It is scarcely the view of Jesus. The traumatic event of AD 70 (Roman destruction of Jerusalem) had scared both the author of 4 Ezra and Matthew. Elsewhere in Matthew when the disciples had questioned Jesus about who can be saved, he had responded: "For mortals it is impossible, but for God all things are possible" (19:23–26). We must constantly remind ourselves that, though we have to think and speak and write of God in anthropomorphic terms, God is *divine*! We speak casually of a God of "infinite love." Do we take the term *infinite* seriously? It is Matthew's view that those who will not find their way through the narrow gate are false prophets. Their fruits will show them up (7:15–20).

The passage 7:21–23 speaks against a hazard of a religious system. The essential demand is to do the will of God. But people can seem to be religious and pious while failing hopelessly to fulfill the revealed will of God as enunciated in the extended teaching of the Sermon. The system had taken over. The wearing of religious titles is no guarantee of true uprightness in the eyes of God. Not everyone who addresses Christ as "Lord" can be assured of partaking in God's reign. Religion must be more than a superficial display. Use of religious language and ritual do not necessarily accomplish the new righteousness and measure up to the moral requirements of the kingdom.

Jesus' words of condemnation are strong and unexpected: "I never knew you; go away from me, you evildoers" (v. 23). "Knowledge," in the Bible, is very often the knowledge of personal relationship. It has overtones of love and attachment: the knowledge that friends have of one another, the mutual knowledge of husband and wife. So Jesus can say, "I never knew you" because those others had not made their contribution to the relationship. They remained aloof by following their own mirage of religious observance. The Sermon concludes with a contrasting parable in verses 24–27. (See also Luke 6:46–49.)

Jesus contrasts the person who responds to his teaching with the one who does not. One who fulfills his words is like a man who built his house on a solid foundation. In the moment of crisis, he can withstand all assaults and temptations because he has made the teaching of Christ the basis of his moral life. But the person who does not act on his teaching cannot claim any such moral integrity or stability. That one is like a man who had built his house on the sandy bed of a river (the dry Palestinian *wadi* or watercourse). When the (winter) floods came, it collapsed under force of flood waters. If a person is to survive the crises of one's moral life, particularly the supreme crisis before the end (the apocalyptic perspective) one must adhere to the teaching of Christ. "*These words of mine*": the authority is no longer the Torah of Moses, but the Law of Christ—including his reinterpretation of Torah.

NOTE

1. G. B. Caird, *Revelation of St John the Divine* (London: A. & C. Black, 1966), 170.

CHAPTER 4

Mission Sermon

BACKGROUND

In chapter 10, Matthew has Jesus sending his disciples on a mission to Israel. Clearly, he wants them to proclaim the good news as he himself had preached it and embodied it. However, before presenting that mission sermon, we have a brief cameo (9:9–13) that captures the graciousness of the Teacher, the mercy of the Savior. It tells them, and us, what the good news is.

> *As Jesus was walking along, he saw a man called Matthew sitting at the tax booth; and he said to him, "Follow me." And he got up and followed him. And as he sat at dinner in the house, many tax-collectors and sinners came and were sitting with him and his disciples. When the Pharisees saw this, they said to his disciples, "Why does your teacher eat with tax-collectors and sinners?" But when he heard this, he said, "Those who are well have no need of a physician, but those*

who are sick. Go and learn what this means, 'I desire mercy, not sacrifice.' For I have come not to call the righteous but sinners."

The compassion of Jesus, manifest in his healings throughout the Gospel, is highlighted in this passage. The scene, Jesus' meal with "tax-collectors and sinners," follows naturally from the call of the tax collector, Matthew. The passage illustrates that Jesus' attitude toward outcasts was a scandal to the more religious-minded. We know that table fellowship (between Christians of Jewish and Gentile backgrounds) was a problem in the early church (cf. Acts 11:3; Gal 2:12), and that it would have been crucial in the matter of Eucharistic table fellowship. It may well be that this interest accounts for the preservation of the original story.

The Pharisees (the "separated ones") regarded Jesus' openly shared meals with tax collectors and sinners—people whose lifestyle surely did not meet proper religious standards—as scandalous behavior. In the Gospels, for historical and political reasons, Pharisees get a bad press. They are cast as legalistic rigorists with little respect and contempt for ordinary folk. This is less than fair. Jesus had a good deal in common with Pharisees. And where, up to the passion narratives, the Gospels might give the impression that the Pharisees were those mainly responsible for the death of Jesus, it was, in fact, the Jerusalem priestly authorities, together with Roman authorities, that engineered the death of Jesus. The prevalent view of Pharisees has exaggerated their political influence and misrepresented their religious outlook. However, given their perception of themselves as people of the Law, they regarded themselves guardians of the Law and of the ancestral customs. Zeal for the Torah became an identity marker of the "sect" of the Pharisees (see Philippians 3:4–6). It is reasonable, then, to take "sinners" as a functional term, describing those whose conduct was regarded as unacceptable to a sectarian mentality.

This brings us back to the conduct of Jesus and to the charge against him. A welcome, on his part, for repentant sinners who had made amends, would have been quite acceptable to the "righteous," whatever else they might have thought of Jesus. The scandal was that he associated with sinners and rejoiced in their company. He did not call them to repent as normally understood, which involved restitution (in personal offences) and a formal offering of sacrifice in the Temple. He asked only that they accept his message, which offered them the kingdom. This was the scandal for the righteous. Jesus preached forgiveness rather than repentance. And he turned forgiveness into celebration (cf. Luke 15).

In dining with tax collectors and "sinners," the pariah elements of the society, Jesus expressed his solidarity with them. Jesus' reply to the objection of the Pharisees, recalling Hosea 6:6, demonstrates that the correct attitude to social dropouts is not one of condemnation and sequestration but of familiarity and service. The Pharisees, who are cast as the hypocrites of Hosea's day, were assiduous in attending the liturgy of the sanctuaries while they ground the faces of the poor. They did not realize that the word "liturgy" means precisely "service," in both senses of the service of God through the liturgy and the service of humans through love. Jesus revealed that these are two sides of the same coin.

The Pharisees' concern with ritual purity should, if it were a matter of true holiness, have pressed them to help the "unenlightened." Jesus' association with the "outlaws" of his day was not tantamount to condoning their actions or situation. Rather, he associated with them in order to raise their sights; to show them a new life. But he could not do this unless he was compassionate toward them.

Against the background of the Old Testament, where Yahweh alone is Physician (see Hos 14:4; Jer 3:22; 17:4; 30:17; Sir 38:1–15) and healing is a sign of the messianic age (see Isa 61:1; Matt 10:1, 8), Jesus' reference to himself as "physician" (Matt 9:12) implies more than a proverbial justification of his conduct: if he eats with sinners it is because the sick have need of the physician. For those who can see, his action is a declaration that the messianic age had dawned; the Physician has come.

The saying of verse 13b, "For I have come not to call the righteous, but sinners," infers that the messianic forgiveness is the basis of table fellowship. The truth was, as the early Christians were well aware, that the saving call of Jesus had been to sinners. It was for this that Jesus had come into the world, to summon such as them to the messianic banquet. This was the comforting assurance addressed to all who have heard the call of Jesus (cf. John 1:8–10). The first Christians knew that the church was made up of sinners.

THE SERMON 9:36—11:1

"A disciple is not above the teacher."
Matthew 10:24

Introduction 9:36—10:4

Sight of a leaderless crowd moves Jesus to think of the need for a mission by his disciples. The kingdom of God has come, the last age, and the mission of bringing the good news to others, of gathering believers into his community, is part of the great final event. It is a task that will challenge Christians while this world lasts. Indeed, we see the harvest-field grow wider and lusher decade by decade. It could be a discouraging task, given the immensity of the harvest (all humankind) and the handful of missionaries. The workers should not yield to discouragement. The Father, the Lord of the harvest, is in control. They should ask him to send out laborers. Prayer becomes a missionary work. But the laborers must not frustrate the work by unwieldy structures and unhelpful rules.

That helpless multitude (9:36) is the backdrop to the choice of twelve disciples (symbol of a renewed Israel) who would continue Jesus' own messianic work. They will alert people to the advent of the kingdom and the availability of salvation. Like Jesus, they too are endowed with the ability to relieve human need, "to cure every disease and every sickness" as a sign and pledge of a more fundamental salvation. They also share Jesus' messianic authority to loosen evil's stranglehold on humankind. For the moment, they are given an apprentice mission. Like Jesus himself (15:24), they are to go only "to the lost sheep of the house of Israel." After the death-resurrection, however, they will be formally commissioned by the risen Lord to undertake a universal mission (28:19).

Noteworthy is the repeated reference to "sheep" (9:36; 10:6). The church's role in the world is that of shepherd or guide. In contemplating the church, people should be able to see God's plan for them. The role of the church is doubly rooted in Christ's compassion for the world and in the church's prayer. It is only by realizing that its work is the channeling of God's mercy and by the continuous opening of itself to this work in prayer that the church will be able to carry out its mission.

Mission to Israel 10:5–15

"I was sent only to the lost sheep of the house of Israel" (15:24). Jesus clearly states the firm limits of the range of his mission. He adhered to the salvation-historical precedence of Israel. His instructions to the Twelve, not surprisingly then, include the same limitation. The mission of the disciples mirrors that of Jesus. The proclamation of the kingdom is the same: "The kingdom of heaven has come near" (see 4:17). They are to cure the sick, raise the dead, cleanse the leper and cast out demons—just as Jesus had done. Significantly, there is no mandate to teach. They can teach confidently only when they have received the full teaching of Jesus; "teaching them to obey *everything* that I have commanded you" (28:20). Because the disciples had received their call and commission and the gifts that went with them "without payment" (v. 8) they must demand no payment. Instead, in their fidelity to mission, they will earn and deserve support (see 1 Cor 9:3–12). "Shake off the dust from your feet" (Matt 9:14): Jews would shake off Gentile dust when they returned from abroad to the Holy Land. Here the point is that those who will not hearken to the gospel (good news) are no better than pagans. The strong language of verse 15 carries a distinctive Matthean theme: judgment is severe for those who have heard the good news but have failed to act upon it.

Emphasis on a mission to Israel was of particular concern to Matthew's community. It viewed itself as the authentic way of Judaism after AD 70, and wanted fellow Jews to see the light. Matthew works on two levels: one is confined to the time and characters of his narrative world (the ministry of Jesus); the other reaches beyond to the person who reads the text through the lens of resurrection faith. This is why, despite the apparent limitation, a mission to the Gentiles is emphatically in place (28:19). A contemporary mission to Israel is not at all excluded. As Daniel Harrington explains,

> Christianity's continuing mission to Israel remains a very delicate matter in Christian-Jewish relations. On the one hand, the mission to the Gentiles (Matt 28:19) does not exclude the mission to Israel (10:5b-6). Indeed, if Christians are convinced of the rightness and importance of the gospel, they are obliged to share it with others, including and especially Jews. On the other hand, the history of the Christian mission to Israel, with its persecutions, forced conversions, and insensitive approaches to

> evangelization, has correctly made most Jews suspicious of such a mission. In its third millennium, Christianity needs to find a better way both to be faithful to the gospel mandate and to be sensitive in its efforts to carry out that mandate.[1]

Trials 10:16–25

"A disciple is not above the teacher, nor a slave above the master" (10:24). The missionaries have been told that they will share the mission and authority of Jesus. Now they are told that they will participate in his persecution and rejection and, it may be, in his death. This is spelled out in 10:17–22, a text which very closely follows Mark 13:9–13. Noteworthy is the threefold repetition of ***paradidomi***, "to deliver up" (vv. 17, 19, 21); persecution and suffering are their lot, serving a divine purpose. They will be hauled before Jewish tribunals (v. 17) and Gentile authorities (v. 18). Paradoxically, as prisoners on trial, they bear witness to the name. They are promised help (vv. 19–20). It is not said that the Spirit will speak up on their behalf. Rather, the help of the Spirit means that the preparation of the defense is less an apologia than a prayer. Most painful of all is the factor of family division (vv. 21–22). This had become a commonplace of apocalyptic literature (e.g., 2 Bar 70:3; 4 Ezra 5:9). Here, however, denunciation from within would suggest the experience of Jewish Christians after AD 70: they found themselves at loggerheads with other family members. The saying of verse 23 envisages an imminent coming of the Son of Man—a prevalent expectation in the early church (cf. Mark 9:1; 13:30). It is not clear how Matthew would have understood it. Verse 25 states the principle underlying the passage: as disciples and slaves, Christians cannot expect a better fate than that of their Teacher and Master.

Trust in God 10:26–33

The missionaries have a role similar to that of Jeremiah and the other prophets, whose successors they are (5:12). For the good news, which they are to preach, is not "good" for everyone. In this passage, towards the end of the mission sermon, Jesus exhorts his disciples to fearless and confident proclamation of the gospel in the teeth of persecution. "Do not fear" is a refrain (vv. 26, 28, 31): the preachers are to fear God only, not human beings; they are to trust in God's care of them. The disciple of Christ must steadfastly proclaim the teaching of the Master and faithfully bear witness to him. The apostle must not fall silent; one may not avoid fearless confession of one's faith. On the contrary, one must seek every opportunity of communicating the saving message of Jesus. One must preach from the housetops and gain the maximum attention for one's words.

These gospel words do not promise the witness of Christ that he or she will escape suffering or even martyrdom. Indeed, all who wish to remain true to the gospel must be prepared to suffer (see 2 Tim 3:12). But the Lord who knows every detail of the lives of his witnesses will take special care of them in every trial and support them in every crisis. If, in their turn, they are faithful, they will meet Jesus' approval at the final tribunal. A warning sounds for one who will have shrunk from bearing witness to Christ: such a one will not be acknowledged as a true child of the Father.

Commitment 10:34–39

Jesus had come to offer peace. Paradoxically, the challenge of his good news brings strife due to rejection of it. Family dissension emerges again: a dramatic presentation of the divisions he occasions. It echoes Micah 7:6. The theme of suffering reemerges (v. 38). Jesus did not shrink from the cross. The faithful disciple will be ready to shoulder it. "Life" (*psyche*) means both "life" and "self." The meaning of the enigmatic saying (v. 19) is that one who, through fear of losing one's (earthly) life, denies Jesus and thus seeks to save oneself, in reality loses one's eschatological life, "eternal life," (John 12:25) with God. It is the paradox of the cross.

Recompense 10:40–42

It is a rabbinical principle that "the representative of a person is as the person." Jesus, as the "one sent," is the Father's representative; the disciples, sent by him, are his representatives. Verse 42 gives the assurance that the smallest act of kindness shown to a disciple will not fail to have its reward. What is presupposed is a gracious God who will not overlook the slightest deed of generosity. "Reward" is not something we earn: it is always the free gift of a generous God. In verses 40–42, it is arguable that Matthew has established an order, which may reflect the structure of his community: we have apostles, ("you"), prophets, the righteous person (a prominent member), and the little ones (the "simple faithful"). Matthew closes the discourse with his customary transitional formula (11:1).

PAUL

A fitting codicil to this mission program is a glance at the experience of the Jewish-Christian missionary Paul. He saw himself, quite rightly, as preeminently an apostle to the Gentiles. But he had a passionate desire for the conversion of his own people to Christ. We have the eloquent testimony of Romans 9—11. The personal cost to Paul of his missionary endeavor was enormous. Most painful was the fierce antagonism of some of his Jewish-Christian fellow workers. It was just such opposition that wrenched from him a vivid listing of his trials in 2 Corinthians 11:23–28.

> We learn from Paul that the cross is a central factor in the Christian way of life, making sense of the otherwise meaningless realities of suffering and death. We learn that, however generously we give ourselves to the task or tasks set out for us, the harvest is never ours, but is always the Lord's (see 1 Cor 3:5–9). This should give us serene confidence. And, when we find that our work for God is blocked by one obstacle or another—a seemingly unintelligible directive, some unexpected opposition, ill-health—and we know discouragement, then we can think of the trials of Paul and

his frustration. Perhaps in that thought we will find comfort.[2]

NOTES

1. Daniel J. Harrington, SJ, *The Gospel of Matthew* (Collegeville: The Liturgical Press. 1991), 143f.

2. Wilfrid J. Harrington, OP, *Seeking Spiritual Growth through the Bible* (New York: Paulist Press, 2002), 102–3.

CHAPTER 5

SERMON IN PARABLES

Chapter 13 is pivotal in the Gospel of Matthew. Just as Jesus used parables to meet the demands of his own situation, so Matthew uses them to meet the needs of his community. The parables of chapter 13 serve Matthew's own age and theology. The parable passage forms the second part of the whole section 11:2—13:53. The first part (chapters 11—12) records the mounting opposition to Jesus and his rejection by the leaders of the people. This is emphasized by the words of thanksgiving for the revelation to "infants" of what remains hidden to "the wise and the intelligent" (11:25–26), and culminates in the passage about the "true relatives" of Jesus; those who do the will of the Father (12:46–50). Then in 13:1–15, Jesus addresses the "crowds" as representing the whole of unbelieving Judaism—those who are blind, deaf, lacking understanding (13:10–13). The first half (13:1–35) of Jesus' parable discussion is an apologia; his reaction to having been rejected by the Jews; the second half of the discourse

(13:36–52) marks a sudden shift to the *disciples* (v. 36). They are such as do God's will (vv. 49–50), and Jesus instructs them as to what doing God's will really means.

PARABLES

Matthew's use of *parable* in chapter 13 conforms to that of Mark in at least two respects. Matthew regards the parable as an enigmatic form of speech directed primarily to outsiders. He distinguishes between a time when Jesus addressed the Jews openly and a time when he begins to address them in parables. In particular, he suggests that Jesus' reply to his rejection by the Jews was distinctively parabolic in form. Jesus had come to the Jews, preaching and teaching, but was rejected by them. He reacted by addressing his apologia to them, but in parables, that is, in riddle, in speech for outsiders. By this fact he proclaims that the Jews are no longer the privileged people of God but, rather, stand under judgment for having spurned their Messiah. This factor (Jesus' turning from the Jews and towards his disciples) is the great turning point of the Gospel; Matthew uses his parable chapter to mark the turning point. But, for him, this is not a matter of past history; it has immediate relevance for the church to which he belongs. It reflects the relationship, one of virulent animosity, between his Jewish Christian community and the contemporary Pharisaic Judaism. While the evangelist does consider the leaders of Judaism to be incorrigible, radically closed to the saving message of Jesus, the same does not hold true of the Jewish people. The people of the Jews may still be evangelized and, as such, the Gospel is addressed to them.

In chapter 13 Matthew calls attention to this turning point in several ways. For one thing, he studiously avoids designating Jesus' speech in parables to the Jews as teaching (*didaskein*) or preaching (*keryssein*); instead he describes it as *lalein*, that is, a "speaking." Furthermore, Matthew consistently refers to the Jewish crowds in 13:1–35 as "them" (*autois*); he thereby depicts the (unbelieving) Jews as a people who stand outside the circle of those to whom God imparts his revelation, and promises his end-time kingdom. He introduces the term *parabole* for the first time in chapter 13, and then distinguishes between a time when Jesus spoke openly to the Jews and a time when he began to speak to them enigmatically. Finally, providing a framework for eight parable units (and two explanations), he drafted a parable speech in two parts.[1]

PART I. 13:1–35

The Sower 13:3–9

Jesus is beside the lake. He uses a boat as his pulpit to address the "great crowds" ranged along the shore (13:1–2). The parable of the Sower (vv. 3–9) might just as well be called the parable of the soils, because throughout, the emphasis is not really on sower or seed but on the different kinds of soil on which the seed falls. As a parable, this is not, as might seem, an agricultural vignette. And the situation depicted is not typically Palestinian as has frequently been suggested. Instead one should take the peculiar actions of the sower as part of the deliberately unusual dimension of the story.

Matthew consistently uses the plural of seed, thus denoting plenty, and he seems to identify "the sower" with Jesus. He uses the parable to recapitulate chapters 11—12, and to validate the denunciation and blessing in 13:10–17. The twin accent on failure and success makes this a parable of contrast. The stress is on verse 8a: the word is continuously manifested in the lives of those who respond. The function of the parable in this context is apologetic and parenetic: it prepares the way for the next passage, which contrasts unbelieving Jews with the disciples.

The Purpose of the Parables 13:10–17

Matthew has an excursus (13:10–17) between the parable of the Sower (vv. 2–9) and its explanation (vv. 18–23). It sets up a sharp contrast between "you" (the Christian community) and "them" (Judaism). They are divided into two estranged camps. Matthew casts the disciples in a favorable light: they are recipients of a special revelation and are the enlightened followers of Jesus. They are not only capable of understanding the parables, but do, in fact, understand them. We may observe the striking contrast between the perplexed attitude of the disciples in Mark 4:10, who "asked him concerning the parables," and their confident bearing in Matt 13:10, where they only wish to know: "Why do you speak to *them* in parables?" For Mark the *unexplained* parable is as much a riddle to the disciples as to the crowd. Therefore, Jesus interprets also for the disciples (cf. Mark 4:34), who he is at pains to underline, and who fail to understand. By contrast, throughout his whole Gospel, Matthew endows the disciples with an insight before Easter, which, in the other Gospels, they do not attain until after Easter. Therefore, the "disciples" in Matthew become representatives of the early Christians.

Matthew (13:13)—"because" (*hoti*) and not "in order that" (*hina*) used by Mark 4:12—does not say that the parable is enigmatic in itself, but he does stress that in order to comprehend it, one must have received from God the capacity to grasp revelation (vv. 11, 16–15). The parable is a riddle only to the crowds; the disciples, precisely because they are disciples, are made recipients of divine insight. Thus they understand the parables of Jesus as a matter of course, and there is no trace of the rebuke of Mark 4:13: "Do you not understand this parable? Then how will you understand all the parables?" Rather, in verses 16–17, the disciples are shown to be of privileged status because of the unique time in which they live—the divine revelation imparted to them, and the glorious promise given them. This is the joyous side of the message. The somber side is that the Jews are a people under judgment. In Matthew, Jesus speaks to them in parables because they are blind, deaf, and without understanding. This supports the circumstances of the context that they have already proved themselves hardened to the Word. *Now* he *begins* to speak in parables.

Explanation of the Sower 13:18–23

The early church's explanation of the parable (vv. 18–23) is concerned with "the word of the kingdom." This word is sown in the hearers. Four categories of hearers are distinguished in terms of the place where the seed has fallen: "on the path," "on rocky ground," "among thorns," and "on good soil." The fate of the word differs in each case. The evil one comes and snatches the word as it is preached (v. 19). Initial joy at the hearing of the word will not compensate for lack of root. Here is a person of the moment, who will not persevere in the face of tribulation and persecution (vv. 20–21). The description of the third person (v. 22) is the analysis of a moralist who leans in great part on the explicit teaching of Jesus. The fourth person (v. 23) suggests that it is enough to be good soil, to be receptive, in order to bring forth fruit. The application is not unfaithful to the parable, for it only takes the subjective aspect of the proclamation and applies it to the hearers. They are shown that the story of the Sower does concern them.

The explanation came about because Christians had discovered to their shock and sorrow that few really believed Jesus' message. They asked the burning question: how could it be that there was such a gulf between themselves and those who could not or would not see? They found an answer in the words of the parable. Think what happens when the sower scatters his seed. Much is lost, for one reason or another. Similarly, many are like the person on the pathway: the word cannot reach them; it is swept away. Or, many prove to be shallow—ready enough to receive, but the readiness did not persist. Many are like seed under thorns; they hear, but the word fights a losing battle against cares and distractions. The shallow mind, the wayward heart, worldly preoccupations, and persecution—are all obstacles that frustrate the growth of faith. The explanation offers a warning and an encouragement (the harvest) to Christians in such conditions.

The Weeds Among the Wheat 13:24–30

This parable picks up the argument of verses 10–17. Grain and weeds grow together. It is Matthew's contemporary situation in which some Jews accepted and others rejected the gospel. How is the situation to be handled? The Lord gives his directive: "Let both of them grow together until the harvest" (v. 30). At the last judgment, God will set matters straight. At times, Matthew seems to forget this recommendation of tolerance. And this is typical of a clash between principle and practice in the religious sphere as in human affairs in general.

One may also read the parable as a description of the church, as a reminder that it is not a community of the elect and eternally secure, but a mixed body of righteous and unrighteous, all of whom stand under the mercy of God. It is a parable of "the kingdom of heaven." The kingdom is not primarily a state or place but rather the dynamic event of God coming in power to rule his people, Israel, in the end-time. However, it should, and can, become a reality here and now. God's rule becomes real when it finds expression in human life. In its present stage, it is not yet ready for harvest; nor has the harvest time arrived. For the present there are good and bad within the kingdom itself. It is only at the judgment that the separation between the two kinds will take place (13:30, 49–50). Emphasis is on the coexistence of good and bad within the kingdom. Because the parable is intended as a repudiation of any elitist or purist view of the kingdom (no "smaller and better" church), it contains a message of hope. As long as the kingdom is growing, it remains possible to change from "weed" into "wheat." For that matter, part of the message of the parable is to exhort the "weeds" to change.

Mustard Seed and Yeast 13:31–33

Between the parable of the weeds and its explanation, Matthew presents two parables with the same message; the contrast between the small, unpromising beginnings of the kingdom (the preaching of Jesus) and a glorious result (the kingdom of God). These parables (vv. 31–32, 33) would have been the answer of Jesus to an objection, latent or expressed: could the kingdom really come from such inauspicious beginnings? His reply is that the little cell of disciples will indeed become a kingdom. And, in the last analysis, if the kingdom does reach its full dimension, it is not due to anything in the men and women who are the seed of the kingdom; the growth is due solely to the power of God (cf. 1 Cor 3:6–7). This is why Jesus can speak with utter confidence of the final stage of the kingdom. And that is why these parables are a call to patience.

Besides, Matthew has an apologetic intent. Contrary to Jewish belief, Jesus declares that the kingdom *has* come in his person, though, because of its humble beginnings, not as they had expected it. He sounds a parenetic note: the Lord fortifies the Christians of Matthew's church in the conviction that they *are* the eschatological community. The words on Jesus' use of parables (vv. 34–35) conclude the first half of Matthew's parable discourse. It anchors Jesus' use of parables in salvation history; the sermon in parables is the fulfillment of prophecy. Jesus thereby testifies to his messiahship and the claim of his church, in his regard, is vindicated.

PART II. FOR THE DISCIPLES 13:36–52

Explanation of the Parable of the Weeds 13:16–43

"Then he left the crowds and went into the house" (13:36). There is a major change of setting. The second part of the parable discourse is directed solely to the disciples. Therefore, Matthew places Jesus in the privacy of a house. The allegorizing explanation of the parable of the weeds (vv. 36–43) is manifestly later than the parable and, very likely, is Matthew's creation. The Lord exhorts the Christians of Matthew's community to be children of the kingdom who do God's will. Here Matthew's ethical concern is bolstered by apocalyptic imagery. The "field" is the "world"; the parable has universal scope. Here the Son of Man is the risen Lord, as in 25:31–46; but the actual agents of judgment are angels. The parable had stressed the need for patient tolerance (v. 30). Matthew has a penchant for looking to fearful judgment. Similarly, the old-style mission, hell-fire sermon was meant to have a salutary effect on the daily lives of the hearers. That the effect was salutary is questionable.

Three Parables 13:44–50

The parables of the treasure and the pearl (vv. 44, 45–46), both closely related and proper to Matthew, are linked by the formula "the kingdom of heaven is like." The key to both is found in the phrase "in his joy" (v. 44). A poor farm laborer had profited from the fate of some wealthy man who, in a moment of crisis, had hidden his valuables but had most likely lost his life. The finder does not hesitate. He has to sell everything he owns—but he *must* have that treasure. The pearl merchant has found what he had dreamt of: the *perfect* pearl. Gladly he sells his caravan or his ship (depending on whether he was a merchant on land or sea) to get that pearl. To an outsider, the conduct of peasant and merchant must seem crazy. Yet *they* know that their course of action is the only one that makes sense. They had discovered the treasure of the kingdom and had realized that it is worth any price. What seems crazy to others is, to them, the only sensible way to act. Note that there is no stress here on sacrifice. Both men gladly give their all because they *know* that they have found so much more.

The parable of the dragnet (vv. 47–50) conveys basically the same message as that of the Weeds (vv. 24–30, 36–41): the kingdom at the present time embraces both "good" and "bad"; it is only at the end that a separation will be made. By placing his emphasis on judgment, Matthew sounds a note of warning.

CONCLUSION

At the end of the discourse (vv. 51–53), the readers are drawn into a parable, one that has to do with understanding. Matthew considers understanding to be essential to the making of a disciple. In Mark, the disciples are devoid of understanding until the resurrection of Jesus. In Matthew, they are true children of the kingdom and understand and accept the message of the kingdom. One who has become a disciple of the kingdom knows and understands both the old (the Old Testament) and the new (the good news) and is in a position to discern God's promises present in the Old Testament and now fulfilled in Christ (which is what Matthew does in his Gospel). At the close, Matthew presents his description of a Christian of his community, who treasures the old (the Jewish heritage) and the new (the good news of and from Jesus). It may, consciously or not, be a self-portrait.

NOTE

1. Jack D. Kingsbury, *The Parables of Jesus in Matthew 13* (London: SPCK, 1969).

CHAPTER 6

SERMON ON THE CHURCH

After the Sermon in Parables (chapter 13), Jesus resumes his ministry in Galilee (13:54–58). From this point on, Matthew follows closely the sequence of Mark. We look at one passage where he has a notable expansion of Mark's text (Mark 8:27–30).

WHO DO YOU SAY THAT I AM? 16:13–20

At Caesarea Philippi, the northern-most limit of historical Israel, Jesus put a leading question to his disciples: "Who do the people take me to be?" They tell him that some who had believed that Elijah had reappeared in John the Baptist now felt that John had returned to life in his successor, Jesus. (For a belief in the return of Elijah, see Malachi 3:1; 4:5.) That he might be Jeremiah or "one of the prophets" simply means that Jesus was a prophetic figure. Jesus brushes aside these views and puts the blunt question to his disciples—and to every believer: "But who do you say that I am?" Peter's answer is, in reality, a Christian confessional formula: "You are the Messiah, the Son of the living God." It goes beyond Mark 8:29 in stressing that Jesus is Son of God in a transcendent sense. The response of Jesus asserts that no human could ever, unaided, understand or communicate the divine mystery of Sonship. Peter had received a revelation.

In a passage proper to Matthew (vv. 18–19), Jesus, who had received titles from Peter, now, in turn, confers a title on Peter: he is "the Rock." And, on the solid foundation of this rock, Jesus' church will be built. (Here and in 18:17 are the only occurrences of *ekklesia* "assembly"—a term used, seemingly, to distance the Matthean community from the Jewish *synagoge*, "synagogue.") The church, the community of salvation, will be preserved from the destructive power of death ("the gates of Hades"); it will last beyond the world. The image of keys (taken from Isaiah 22:15–25) invests Peter with the power of vicegerent. He will have the authority to decide, according to the teaching of Jesus, what is permissible and what is not, and the authority—always, of course, on truly Christian principles—to admit members to the community or, if need be, to exclude them.

Since the Sermon in Parables, Matthew had been concerned with the delineation of the kingdom of heaven. It is a mysterious, divine reality. Its beginnings are humble, indeed, compared with its future glory. Nonetheless, the kingdom has concrete expression in the world. People are nourished within it; they embrace it in the hope of healing and divine protection. The question arises: What is the kingdom? Here that question is rephrased, "Who do people say that the Son of Man is?" The evangelist tells us that it is not "What is the kingdom?" but "Who is the kingdom?" that is important. When we ask the question about Jesus aright, then we get the kingdom right. Jesus embodies the kingdom; everything about it refers to himself. All power in the kingdom is invested in Christ. Its authentic movements, energy, and position flow from him. Once the faith of Peter has opened the apostle's heart to Jesus and so brought one into the kingdom, the kingdom's power can flow into one, and, from Jesus' own lips, it flows into one in a special manner. Equally clearly, Jesus' promise to Peter is not about privilege to possess as much as duty to perform. Jesus transforms *exousia*, authority, into *diakonia*, service. If *service* is not recognizably the pattern of authority in the church at every level, then authority loses credibility.

If the text of Matthew 16:18–19 were to be highlighted in isolation from counterbalancing features of New Testament ecclesiology—on brother/sisterhood, mutual service, humility, diversity of charisms, and so on—it would result in distortion and diminish personal dignity within the church. Besides, the New Testament is not in agreement as to the foundation of the church. For example, 1 Cor 3:11 states that "No one can lay any other foundation than the one that has been laid; that foundation is Jesus Christ." However, according to Ephesians 2:20, the household of God is "built upon the foundation of the apostles and prophets, with Christ Jesus himself as the cornerstone." Then there is the declaration of the seer of Revelation: "The wall of the city [the new Jerusalem] has twelve foundations, and on them the names of the twelve apostles of the lamb" (21:14); the "city" is a people living in the presence of God.

SERMON ON THE CHURCH: CHAPTER 18

This Sermon falls into two parts: care of the "little ones" (vv.1–14), and the treatment of a community member who sins (vv. 15–35). Each part ends with a parable—the Lost Sheep (vv. 10–14) and the Unforgiving Servant (vv. 23–35).

True Greatness 18:1–7

The disciples had questioned Jesus: "Who is the greatest in the kingdom of heaven?" Their question and Jesus' response suggest that we are already on the road to ecclesiasticism, with a "hierarchy" and a "simple faithful" (see 23:1–12). Throughout the Sermon, Matthew is concerned with life within the Christian community. The audience is "the disciples," and the address is primarily to community leaders. Matthew omits Mark's lively action parable (Mark 9:36) but makes the same point. There is no place for degrees of greatness among disciples of Jesus: the least disciple of Jesus has greatness. Whoever receives a child for the sake of Jesus receives Jesus and, in turn, receives the God who sent him. The greatness that comes from belonging to Jesus, from being his disciple, can be enjoyed by a child. Jesus is not establishing the authority of his disciples over others but is pointing out the greatness of discipleship—there is no greater dignity. It follows that ecclesiastical office is, above all, a *service*. This is seen more clearly in Mark 8:35: "Whoever wants to be first must be last of all and servant of all." There is no "first" in the reign of God. Jesus leaves little space for ambition; no room for the exercise of power.

Care of the "Little Ones" 18:1–14

The "child" of verses 1–5 suggests the "little ones" of verses 6–7. "These little ones who believe in me": the humblest, most vulnerable members of a Christian community. "Put a stumbling block" is a warning on the grievousness of the sin of those who lead simple Christians astray by callously shaking their faith. Those who propose a merciless God are most gravely at fault. "A great millstone" is, literally, a "donkey millstone," that is, a millstone turned by a donkey, in contrast to the smaller millstone worked by a woman (see Matt 24:41). Death by drowning was a Roman punishment and was particularly repugnant to Jews due to the lack of a proper burial. The warning, then, is very sharp.

The two sayings in verses 8 and 9, linked by the catchword *scandalize*, are about scandal. However, not in terms of those who place a stumbling block before others, but in reference to whatever within oneself can cause one to stumble and fall into sin. There is no question, obviously, of actual mutilation, but the vivid Semitic idiom enjoins, in the starkest terms, the costliest sacrifice. The "Gehenna (hell) of fire"—originally Gehenna, the valley of the son of Hinnom—was a ravine south of Jerusalem where infants were sacrificed to Moloch (Jer 7:31; 10:5–6; 39:35). It was desecrated by Josiah (2 Kgs 23:20) and was henceforth used as a dump for offal and refuse. Jeremiah warned that, there, the faithless ones of Israel would be destroyed by fire. As a site of ill omen, it came to symbolize the place of final punishment (see 4 Ezra 7:36; Enoch 27:2). The "hell of fire"—only crass literalism could have led to the later notion of hell as a place of fiery torment. And to a God who condemns sinners to that hell: blasphemy by any decent standard.

The Lost Sheep 18:10–14

In Luke 15:4–7, the parable of the Lost Sheep is an explicit answer to the murmuring of the Pharisees and scribes: "This fellow welcomes sinners and eats with them." The same parable occurs in Matthew. Here it is no longer addressed to opponents of the good news but to disciples. The discourse of which it forms part ends: "it is not the will of your Father that one of these little ones should be lost" (18:14). Even if the application were not already clear, the context clinches the issue. The warning not to despise one of the least (v. 10) and the subsequent admonition regarding fraternal/sisterly correction (vv. 15–17) leave no doubt about the meaning of verse 14: It is God's will that you go after the erring brother or sister, the weak and helpless one, as earnestly as the shepherd of the parable sought out the lost sheep. It would seem that Luke had preserved the original setting of the parable: Jesus' response to the charge that he was a "friend of sinners." When one thinks about it, what could be a more appropriate designation of the Son of God; Son of a God who, outrageously, when one reads the Old Testament correctly, has a preferential option for sinners!

The change of audience in Matthew is readily explained. Early Christians sought in this, as in other parables, a message that met their needs and they took it as applying to themselves. In acting so, they had not forced its message. The Lost Sheep was spoken to justify the concern shown by Jesus for sinners and outcasts. The Christian, to be like the Master, should manifest solicitude for the confused brother or sister. There is, simply, a shift of emphasis: an apologetic parable has taken on a hortatory thrust.

Reproving Another Who Sins 18:15–20

This passage has to do with brotherly/sisterly correction. To be properly evaluated, it needs to be read in the context of a chapter that declares the greatness of a childlike sense of littleness (vv. 1–5), insists on loving care of weak members of a Christian community (vv. 6–14), and is certain that the Christian word, first and last, must be forgiveness (vv. 21–35). In this setting, the seemingly harsh demand of excommunication (v. 17) appears in a *Christian* light. The brother or sister contemplated in our passage is not the "little one" of verse 6, nor the weak, candid sinner of verse 21. It is one who may prove intransigent. What is important is that Matthew outlines a precisely articulated procedure, a procedure inspired by the Old Testament but which takes on a distinctively Christian flavor. Clearly he has in mind Leviticus 19:17–18: "You shall not hate in your heart any one of your kin; you shall reprove your neighbor…but you shall love your neighbor as yourself," and Deuteronomy 19:15: "Only on the evidence of two or three witnesses shall a charge be sustained."

The first point Matthew makes is that, within a Christian community, one does not start by "passing the buck," by planting the problem straight on the leader's desk. The proper procedure is to approach *privately* the erring brother or sister. If the intervention succeeds, that is the end of the matter, and one has the joy of winning over a brother or sister. If another attempt becomes necessary, it is still a private matter involving only two or three community members. If this fails, only then is the whole community to take up formally the case of an obstinate sinner. From first to last, it is a community concern. And, if it has to come to it, it is the community that excommunicates.

In the Judaism of Jesus' day, a "Gentile" was a pagan outsider and a "tax collector" was a traitor. Matthew's largely Jewish-Christian community would have inherited such a characterization but would have gone on to regard a "Gentile" as the non-Christian and "tax-collector" as one who can no longer be called Christian. The community, vulnerably human as it is (see 1 Cor 5:6) must protect itself against the threat from within as well as from without. All the while, a prime concern must be the (eternal) welfare of the sinner. If the sinner repents—and that is the hope—then forgiveness must be warm and without limit or condition (Matt 18:21–22). Each and every Christian, because he or she has encountered a forgiving Father, would be eager to forgive (18:23–25).

In their present context, verses 18–20 mean that the verdict of the community (if arrived at in a truly Christian way) will be ratified by God. In verse 18, the power to bind and loose, previously bestowed on Peter (16:19) is now given to the community. Originally, it is clear that these sayings had to do with *prayer*. And there is the assurance that where Christians (even two or three) gather in Jesus' name, he is with them—he is Emmanuel, God-with-us (cf. 1:23; 28:20). In verse 18, "binding" and "loosing" would refer to the imposition or lifting of decrees of excommunication. Surely there is always the supposition that the grave matter of disciplining a brother or sister is never a question of "throwing the book" at one. It has to be a *prayerful* decision. Otherwise, while it may stand as a decision, it will not stand as a Christian deed.

Forgiveness 18:21–35

Just as ben Sirach regards the forgiveness of our neighbor as crucially important for right human conduct (Sir 28:2–4), so Matthew underlines its significance for the early church. This passage forms the conclusion of his Sermon on the Church. Though he had to face the uncomfortable fact that an unrepentant brother or sister might have to be excluded from the community (vv. 15–20), he wants to ensure that his word on relationships within the community will end on the resounding note of forgiveness. While Luke (17:4) also provides the saying about forgiveness, Matthew adds special importance to it in three ways: by putting the question in the mouth of Peter, leader of the Christian community; by increasing the number of times from seven (already the perfect number signifying "any number of times") to seventy-seven (or, seven times seven)—an unlimited number of times; and by adding a parable, as he likes to do at the end of a passage to drive the point home.

The disparity between the two sums mentioned in the parable is gigantic—ten thousand talents is an unimaginable sum. (A talent was the highest currency unit; denarius, a workman's daily wage.) A debt impossible to repay is written off casually by the king, and the man is not even fired. It is quite the situation one finds in Luke 15:11–24. Yet, one who had been shown such mercy cannot find it in his heart to remit a paltry sum. Not only that, he will not even give his fellow servant—his social equal—reasonable time and opportunity to repay. The king, who had been moved with "pity" (v. 27), is now "angry" (v. 34).

The parable is a thinly veiled allegory. The "servant" is the sinner; his situation is hopeless. The "king" is a merciful God who freely and lovingly forgives any sin. Luke has painted the warmer picture of prodigal Father and wayward child (15:11–24). The reality is the same in either case. Like the younger son in the Lukan parable, this man, too, is forgiven with no strings attached. Faced with a cry of desperation, the forgiving God was moved with pity (Matt 18:27). But when the recipient of such forgiveness cannot find it in his heart to be merciful, the Master is angry (v. 33)—"anger" being righteous indignation. Response to God's gracious forgiveness cannot be payment of a debt that is already fully remitted. Instead, it is warm thanksgiving for the blessing of such forgiving love (cf. Luke 7:36–50). The story in Matthew underlines again that sin, as God regards it, is man's inhumanity to man (even more sadly, man's inhumanity to woman), whatever shape that may take. Our abuse of others (and of ourselves) is an affront to the loving Father who counts us as his children. Jesus clearly understood this because he knew his Father. As a corollary, Jesus asks us, frail humans, to be forgiving, without limit. He dares to ask the impossible because he knew that his God is an Abba whose forgiveness literally knows no limit.

The implications of Matt 18:15–35 for life within the Church today are great. The text outlines a clear procedure designed to help the sinner recognize the sin and return to the community. It roots reconciliation and forgiveness of sins in God's mercy, and thus reveals the foolishness of those who try to set limits on their willingness to forgive others.[1]

NOTE

1. Daniel J. Harrington, SJ, *The Gospel of Matthew* (Collegeville, MN: The Liturgical Press, 1991), 272.

CHAPTER 7

TOWARD THE PASSION

"When Jesus had finished saying these things, he left Galilee and went to the region of Judea beyond the Jordan" (Matt 19:1). The Gospel is moving towards its climax. Accordingly, we now look to the lead up to the Judgment Sermon.

MOUNTING OPPOSITION

What Jesus meant by God's reign—the rule of God—has been succinctly expressed by the author of the letter to Titus: "When the goodness and loving kindness of God our Savior appeared, he saved us not because of any works of righteousness that we had done, but according to his mercy" (Titus 3:4–5). The God of Jesus is a God who has supreme concern for people. His Lordship points to an ideal, God-willed relationship between God and humanity. Jesus lived and died for the establishment of that rule. He ached for men and women to discover the love of God for humankind and give substance to the wonder of the discovery through loving concern for one another. That love would involve sacrifice and suffering, as it did for Jesus. Opposition to Jesus is visible throughout the Gospel. Now it becomes more bitter and more threatening. Still, Jesus' message, despite an increased note of warning, continues to be one of hope and promise. The negative tone issues not from Jesus, but from a Matthew faced with community problems. We should be confident that Jesus revealed the Abba, the wondrous Hebrew God of *infinite* love. The narrative of Matthew 19—23 is interspersed with parables. In keeping with the emphasis of this book on Jesus as teacher, we will concentrate on these parables.

LABORERS IN THE VINEYARD 20:1–16

A major difficulty in interpreting the parables of Jesus is that we can never be sure when, where, nor in what circumstances Jesus spoke a parable. The setting provided by an evangelist usually reflects his own concern. It is evident that Matthew intends the parable of the laborers in the vineyard (proper to him) to be understood in close connection with Jesus' promise of reward to his disciples (19:27–30). It is just as clear that the parable does not fit smoothly into that context. For Jesus, the parable surely has to do with God's generosity, which transcends human standards.

The saying "So the last will be first and the first will be last" (v. 16) is certainly not the conclusion of the original parable. It is an independent and floating logion (see 19:30;

Mark 10:31; Luke 13:30). We can even see why it was added in Matthew. Verse 8b, "Call the laborers and give them their pay, beginning with the last and then going to the first," seemed to represent a reversal of rank that would take place at the judgment and the saying would appear to be perfectly in place. But it is so only at first sight because the wage is still the same in each case. Besides, verse 8b may be rendered quite accurately: "Pay them their wages, including the last as well as the first."

The parable, then, originally ended at verse 15, and the key to it is in the last phrase of the verse: "because I am generous." It is this goodness that explains the apparently capricious conduct of the householder. For, indeed, at first sight, it does seem unfair that all the workers were to receive the same wage. Yet, when we understand his motive, we judge his conduct very differently. A denarius represented a day's wage, just enough to support a family; anything less, and especially payment for a single hour, would be inadequate. These are laborers, waiting for someone to employ them. They are not his employees; he has no obligation in their regard. What he has in their regard is concern. It is because he had pity on them that the owner called them to his vineyard in the first place, and it is because he has pity on them that he pays all a full wage. There is nothing arbitrary in his conduct; it is the action of a man full of compassion for the poor. So, too, does God act, for God is all goodness and mercy. This is the message of the parable.

However, if we look at the parable again, we shall see that it is two-pronged, that it is made up of two episodes. First we have the hiring of the laborers and instruction about their payment (vv. 1–8), and then the indignation of the recipients who feel themselves cheated (vv. 9–15). It is characteristic of such parables that the emphasis falls on the second part. Because that is so here, we should realize that the parable is aimed at people who resemble the murmurers. The fact is that God is not "fair"! The parable shows what God is like, full of compassion for the poor. It points out how wrong-headed it is to be scandalized by his great goodness. Matthew is hitting at those who bear a grudge within his community. God's prodigal goodness is an affront to human level-headedness. God's love of sinners is an insult to the pious. We find a similar message in Luke's parable of the Prodigal Father (Luke 15:11–32). The elder son (the "righteous") resents the mercy of the father (vv. 25–32).

THE TWO SONS 21:28–32

Throughout the Gospel, Matthew points out that by rejecting and killing the Son, Israel brought about its own rejection. The Gentiles have received the kingdom, which Israel has forfeited. Our parable of the Two Sons (proper to Matthew) is directed explicitly against the Jews, and Jesus puts their own condemnation in the mouths of his accusers (vv. 30–31). As so often, the vineyard (following Isa 5) stands for Israel, God's chosen people, and the contrast is made between the seemingly obedient sons of the father, the "righteous" Jews, and those whom Jesus' hearers regarded as contemptible outcasts. On the face of it, they refuse what is required of them because they do not observe the Law, but they in fact please God more by their openness and love. The point of the parable is that the Jewish leaders, who have promised to work for God but have failed to do so, will be rejected. "I go, sir" (v. 30); *kyrios* is "sir" or "Lord." This son is one who says, "Lord, Lord" but does not do the will of the Father (7:21). Others who have said "No" to God at first (the tax collectors and the prostitutes, for example) but have afterwards repented and done his will, are received into God's kingdom. The reaction of the first son is a key factor in the parable: he "changed his mind"—thought better of his initial refusal. What we profess to believe has no value if it is not translated into active obedience (see 7:21–27). The warning is addressed to "religious" people in every age.

THE WICKED TENANTS 21:33–43

The motifs of vineyard and son link this parable to the preceding one (21:28–32). Together with 21:1–14, they form a series of three parables illustrating the Jewish leaders' refusal of the kingdom and thus Israel's threatened loss of privilege as God's chosen people. The background of this parable is clearly Isaiah 5:1–7, except here there is a distinction between "vineyard" and "tenants." The "landowner's" contention is not with the "vineyard" (that is, Israel) but with the "tenants" (that is, the Jewish leaders). In fact, this parable, along with the other two, is addressed to "the chief priests and elders of the people" (21:23, 28, 45; 22:1). They recognized that they were being addressed (v. 45).

We are dealing with an allegory: The landowner is God; the vineyard is Israel; the wicked tenants are the religious leaders of Israel; the servants are the prophets; the son is Jesus, and the son's death is his crucifixion outside Jerusalem (see Heb 13:13–14). The reference in verse 42 to Psalm 118:22–23 pinpoints Jesus' triumph in his resurrection, not merely in spite of, but precisely because of his rejection by contemporary Jewish leaders. Unwittingly, the tenants were right when they said: "This is the heir, come let us kill him and get his inheritance" (v. 38). Paradoxically, it was only through being rejected by people and being vindicated by God that Jesus became the Savior not alone of the nations but also of Israel. In verse 43 the Jewish leaders are told that they will be replaced by "a people that produces the fruits of the kingdom"—the leaders of the Jewish Christian community. Verse 41 has in mind the fate of Jerusalem in AD 70. There was a tendency to view the destruction of the city as God's judgment on the rejection of the Son.

The parable also functions as a theological explanation of the death of Jesus. Jesus was "delivered up" to death; he was "handed over according to the definite plan and foreknowledge of God" (Acts 2:22). What does this mean? The parable gives the answer. The Son knew the Father and came to do his will. His life was not laid down in response to divine need. It was laid down in answer to divine love. Father and Son were prepared to go to any length to save us humans from ourselves. "Surely, they will respect my Son!" The death of Jesus was, ultimately, the sacrifice made by the Father. Paul had got it right: "He who did not withhold his own Son, but gave him up for all of us, will he not with him also give us everything else?" (Rom 8:32).

ROYAL WEDDING BANQUET 22:1–14

Drawing inspiration from Isaiah 25:6–10, among other passages, Jesus' contemporaries envisaged the arrival of God's reign in terms of a banquet, an eschatological celebration. Jesus addressed his parable of the Wedding Banquet (see Rev 19:9) to those people (in the present context, the chief priests and leaders of the people) who consider that, belonging to Israel, they have no need to reply to the invitation in order to enter the banquet of the kingdom; they have reserved places. Emphasis is on the invitation and its acceptance or rejection. Like the vineyard (Matt 21:28–32, 33–43), the banquet is a metaphor. If the former image brings out the "fruit-bearing" aspect of the kingdom, the latter emphasizes both its joy and the need to respond to God's call when he invites people to enter. In reaction to the rejection of his invitation, "the king sent his troops, destroyed those murderers, and burned their city" (v. 7). Reference to the destruction of Jerusalem in AD 70 is more obvious than previously in 21:41. Again, Matthew echoes that early interpretation of the event: it happened because the leaders of Israel rejected the invitation to the kingdom and maltreated the messengers—especially Jesus. Once again, we see that sad human penchant for depicting God as, somehow vindictive. In verses 8–10, the gathering of all and sundry refers to the Christian mission.

Matthew's final scene (vv. 11–13) is really a second parable combined with the first. (This explains the incongruity that people dragged in off the street [v. 10] are blamed for not being properly dressed for a wedding [v. 12].) It is Matthew's warning to the church. The church is held together neither by family ties nor by an external structure, but by the active, personal, and continual response to God's word. The response is the work of a lifetime. The "wedding robe" of verses 11–12 is a symbol of this response; that is, of a life lived in conformity with God's word as it has been revealed in Christ. The condemnation of verse 13 is a warning to Christians that they, too, like the religious leaders of Israel, can fail to answer God's invitation. The observation of verse 14 (which does not really fit verses 1–10 or 11–13) does suit Matthew's general intention—a reminder of the need to respond to God's call. God's invitation is to all ("many") but only those who truly respond will become the chosen, the elect. Mere membership of the church is not enough. Response is in doing the will of the Father (7:21). Happily, God and the Son are always more gracious than those who speak in their name.

ATTEMPTED ENTRAPMENT 22:15–40

Matthew 22:15–21 is the first of three attempts (see 22:23–33, 34–40) on the part of Jesus' adversaries "to entrap him in what he said." The present ruse is obvious. By and large the Pharisees were anti-Roman while the Herodians (supporters of the dynasty of Herod) were pro-Roman. The question of the legitimacy of paying taxes to Rome was a lively one for Jesus' contemporaries. Jesus is faced with a dilemma: "Is it lawful to pay...or not?" If he were to answer "yes," he would lose the esteem of the people and be discredited as a traitor to the Jewish cause of independence from Rome. If he were to answer "no," he could be denounced as fomenting rebellion. Rome regarded refusal to pay taxes as tantamount to rebellion.

Jesus cleverly evaded the trap by asking his questioners for a denarius, the Roman coin used to pay the poll tax (the tax in question here). They promptly produced one. He had scored a point: they, ostensibly so concerned about the implication of the tax, thereby conceded that they carried and used Caesar's money. By using Caesar's money, he implied, they tacitly accepted his imperial system and should be prepared to pay his taxes. Give back to him, then, what is his: "Give therefore to the emperor the things that are the emperor's." Jesus went on to declare: "And to God the things that are God's." He can hardly mean that there are some things that belong to Caesar and others which belong to God, as if reality were divisible into "secular" and "sacred." What he means is that an obligation to Caesar stands under and is judged by a paramount obligation to acknowledge the sovereignty of the supreme Sovereign.

This classic pronouncement story, which manifestly builds up to the pronouncement in verse 21, offers no neat solution to the question of church-state relations. The legitimate state has rights and the good citizen will respect them. For the Christian, there may come a time when one must hearken to the supreme Sovereign rather than to the state.

Jesus has given a principle but, like so much of his teaching, it has to be practiced in situations that are not at all clear. Christians and the Church must so often be content to live with uncertainty.

In 22:23–33, the Sadducees poured ridicule on the "new-fangled" doctrine of the resurrection of the body. Jesus pointed out that they were mistaken on two counts: in their view that Scripture was Pentateuch only, and in their failure to understand the power of God, who is capable of achieving something beyond human imagining and, in particular, make resurrection life something different from and higher than life in this world. Jesus, in fact, presented the current more sophisticated, as opposed to the popular notion of resurrection. Paul's teaching in 1 Corinthians 15:35–50 is a good formulation of the same view.

In Matthew 22:34–40, there is a third attempt to "entrap Jesus in what he said" (cf. 22:15). By rabbinical count, the "law" comprised 613 commandments, thus providing the scribes with the question about the greatest commandment. The aim of the question addressed to Jesus was to have him commit himself in a much-debated topic, and thus make it possible for the "crowds" (21:46) to be divided about him. Evading the trap, Jesus pinpointed as the greatest commandment what is not, strictly speaking, a commandment at all, but rather the "soul" of all the commandments: the love of God.

In reply to his questioner, Jesus quoted Deuteronomy 6:4–5, the heart of the *Shema*, a prayer recited morning and evening by observant Jews. But he did not stop there. He went on to make this "abstract" commandment very concrete and practical by quoting also Leviticus 19:18: "You shall love your neighbor as yourself." What is new is not the bringing of these commandments together but the making them of equal weight and importance. What is more, Jesus declared (v. 40) that all the laws of the Old Testament and all the preaching of the prophets—the whole of God's revelation—"hang upon" these two commandments as upon a double peg. Jesus did not spell out the relationship between the two commandments. He left it for Paul (Rom 13:8–10) and John (John 13:34) to show that, in fact, they are not two commandments but one: the love of God in the love of one's neighbor.

STYLE OF AUTHORITY 23:1–12

Conflict between the Jewish authorities and Jesus is well documented in the Gospels. But Mathew 23 is something special. As it stands, it is an indictment of Pharisaic Judaism painfully reflecting the bitter estrangement of church and synagogue towards the close of the first century AD. Here we have a thoroughgoing rejection of Pharisaic Judaism by Matthew and his community. This accounts for the harshness of the Matthean Jesus' tirade. It would seem that the earliest Matthean community saw itself as an exclusive reform movement within Judaism and regarded itself as more observant than the Pharisees. This explains the otherwise surprising statement: "The scribes and the Pharisees sit on Moses' seat, therefore do whatever they teach you and follow it; but do not do as they do" (23:2–3). It is an echo from that first period when the Matthean group saw itself as going beyond the meticulous Pharisaic observance of Torah. Elsewhere, Matthew has firmly rejected Pharisaic teaching (15:1–20; 16:1–12) and in this chapter he rejects their practices in verses 5–10 and their teaching in verses 16–20.

At the same time, Matthew uses "scribes and Pharisees" as an example of the negative side of Christian leadership: "Jesus said to the crowd *and to his disciples*" (23:1). In 23:1–7, Jesus castigates the Pharisees and scribes in the third person—"they." Then, in 23:8–12, he switches to the second person—"you," where he addresses the church. We discern an ironical twist in Matthew's graphic narrative of Jesus' denunciation of those who hold authority in the synagogue. He is concerned that, in his day, Jesus' followers have developed attitudes and behavior reminiscent of those "scribes and Pharisees." In depicting Jesus' staunch rejection of such conduct, he unmasks the problematic character of leadership in Christian communities.

The Pharisees are criticized because their interpretation of the Law takes little account of human frailty and tends to be more severe than humane (v. 4). They are people who make custom their dictator, vanity and ostentation their lifestyle. Showing off, parading piety, enjoying the limelight, insisting upon places of honor—such are forms of play-acting, incredible performances in the name of religion (vv. 5–7). How painfully representative of ecclesiastical style, even in our day! Is there really any justification for silly titles and bizarre garb? Matthew's word to leaders in his community is that you must remember that you are *servants* of the community. You must avoid the titles "rabbi," "father," "teacher." The title Rabbi, literally, "my great one," would sit incongruously on one who is "slave" of the community, nor is anyone to be addressed as "teacher," practically the same as "rabbi." Already, by Matthew's day, religious leaders were seeking to be "real" leaders!

True religion, as taught and exemplified by Jesus, is a family-of-God affair, characterized by simplicity, affection, brother/sisterhood (vv. 8–12). He was insisting—and this is what his followers were meant to be aware of—that the teacher is the minister and servant of God's word to the people. There is only one Father, God, and all people are brothers and sisters. There should not be an insistence on privilege and on exercise of power that distorts this relationship.

SEVEN WOES 23:13–36

Jesus had prefaced his first discourse with the Beatitudes (5:3–12), promising eternal happiness to the poor and marginalized who suffer now. As a prelude to the final discourse, he threatens eternal woe to those who pride themselves on their own righteousness. Jesus had indeed been critical of the Judaism of his contemporaries. In this polemic of chapter 23, Matthew targets the leadership of the Jewish community in bitter conflict with his Jewish Christian community. He characterizes them as "hypocrites." The Greek term *hypocrites*, designates an actor who performs behind a mask. For Matthew, these "scribes and Pharisees"—leaders of the early rabbinic movement—wear masks of righteousness. There is in them a fatal split between saying and doing, between appearance and reality. To cap it all, they are arrogant and heartless legalists. His "woes" express his dismay at the situation and carry a threat of punishment. They are couched in the uninhibited language of polemic.

The seven woes might be paraphrased:

Woe to you scribes and Pharisees. You are hypocrites: externally strict observers of the law; inwardly corrupt. Woe to you:

- Because you shut the door of the kingdom of heaven and prevent people from entering;
- Because you travel over sea and land to win one convert—and then make him a bigger hypocrite than yourselves;
- Because you say: To swear by the Temple gold is binding—not an oath by the Temple! To swear by the gift on the altar is binding—not an oath by the altar! Surely, the altar is greater than the gift, the Temple greater than its gold! And one who swears by the Temple is swearing by the One who dwells there;
- Because you tithe the most insignificant of garden herbs—and ignore the real matters of the Law: justice, mercy, faith. You legalists, straining out gnats and gulping a camel!

- Because you clean the outside of cup and dish, and leave the inside full of robbery and self-indulgence—very images of yourselves!

- Because you are like whitewashed tombs: outwardly upright; inside full of hypocrisy and crime;

- Because you venerate the martyred prophets; you sons of their murderers! Finish off what your fathers began—by murdering the Son of Man!

The holy city had rejected the eschatological—the last—prophet (vv. 37–39). There is no recovery from this rejection; there will be no other prophet. These leaders will encounter their rejected Messiah next time on the day of judgment. Then they will recognize him, but too late. Israel had its chance and had failed. In view of the "woes" and the awesome declaration of 27:25 (seen as fulfillment of the word of 23:35–36), one must be alert to the whole of the New Testament message and, above all, sensitive to the startlingly new teaching of Jesus. Not only later Christians, but also New Testament Christians found it hard or impossible to live up to his ideal. His challenge still rings out to all who will listen. The God of Jesus is ever the Father of infinite love, of unbounded forgiveness.

CHAPTER 8

JUDGMENT SERMON

When Matthew wrote his Gospel (around AD 90), the Jerusalem temple had long been destroyed (in AD 70). He predicts its end and an outline of the sufferings of the Jewish war (AD 66–70) because he hopes that he can thereby help Christians to respond adequately to their present difficulties. The first part of Matthew's discourse follows Mark 13 very closely, though with typical modifications. Jesus had spoken a word against the temple in 23:38. Now as he leaves it, he speaks plainly of its total destruction (24:1–2). Then, seated on the Mount of Olives, he turns to the group of disciples.

The topic of interest in their question (24:3) is not the end of the temple but the time of the Lord's *parousia* and the end of the world. Jesus does not answer the question directly; instead he starts to warn of the "birth pangs"—a traditional term to express the view that the messianic age would come to birth amidst a period of woes. It will be a time of false prophets and pseudo-messianic claimants. War and famine denote the Jewish war but, in apocalyptic style, point beyond to the cosmic events to come. The next stage figures in verses 9–14—the tribulation of the church: suffering coming from within and from without. A hostile world will *deliver up* the disciples to death: Christians will be hated and persecuted because of the name—the person—of Jesus. More dreadful is the prospect of betrayal and apostasy fostered by mischief-making prophets. All is not lost. Some will endure faithfully to the end and win salvation. They are those who, in face of troubles from within and from without, will steadfastly proclaim "the good news of the Kingdom," the good news of the triumphant coming of God's reign. Only with this universal proclamation of the gospel will the end be at hand.

False messianic claimants and false prophets must have been a bother for Matthew's church, because they emerge again to heighten the alarming picture of the last days (vv. 23–28). These false prophets may make appeal to the Christ of their own desire and imagining but there is the comfort that they will not succeed in leading astray faithful Christians. There will be challenges, too, from messianic and esoteric circles outside the Christian body. However, when the Son of Man comes, it will be as suddenly and as visibly as a bolt of lightning. Thus any who claim secret knowledge of his coming must not be heeded.

The question of 24:3 is answered: the parousia of the Son of Man and the close of the age will follow immediately on the great tribulation (vv. 29–31). The cosmic signs that accompany the parousia are part and parcel of Jewish apocalyptic descriptions of the Day of the Lord. The Son of Man will come in glory, riding triumphantly on the clouds of heaven. With supreme authority, but with graciousness, the Son of Man will gather his elect—they belong to him. This gathering will be the last task of his angels, those "ministering spirits, sent out to serve those who are to inherit salvation" (Heb 1:14).

WATCHFULNESS 24:36—25:46

The tone of the second part of the discourse (24:36—25:46) is emphatically that of moral exhortation. It opens with three short parables on vigilance (vv. 36–44). Some Christians were overeager for the parousia (v. 36), while others were indifferent to it or were leading lives of careless unreadiness. They are warned that judgment is imminent. A carefree business-as-usual was typical of the contemporaries of Noah; what they were doing was not wrong in itself, but they had no thought of God. The end was sudden and unexpected and their heedlessness left them unprepared. People will be judged as individuals and not in batches (vv. 40–41). Two men (or two women) will not necessarily share the same judgment simply because they work at the same occupation. One will be taken, the other left (as one was taken aboard the ark, for salvation, another left behind, for destruction). Warning of the return of Jesus like a thief in the night prepares for the moral: "You must be prepared in the same way." The theme of the future soft-footing into the present like a burglar appears elsewhere in the New Testament (1 Thess 5:2–4; 2 Pet 3:10). The only preparation possible, the only preparation necessary, is our constant care to live in the light and love of the Lord made human for us. When Matthew wrote his Gospel, the old Israel was already devastated. This does not mean that the church can now forget about judgment. But judgment will not be as dramatic as in the majestic scene of Matthew 25. The "second coming" is a powerful statement of the completeness of God's saving plan for humankind. Alertness is all the more emphasized because this evangelist has a developed consciousness of the length of time that must elapse before the "coming." Hence, the warnings to the lukewarm and the demand for watchfulness!

The three short parables of vigilance are followed by three longer ones. The first, the Faithful or the Unfaithful Slave (24:45–51) is aimed specifically at church leaders. They are urged to be prudent and faithful in their caring for the community. The danger is that the leader who lacks a sense of urgency will forget that he is a servant and begin to lord it over others. For Matthew the "hypocrites" are the Jewish leaders. The unfaithful Christian leader is no better than they and will come under a like condemnation.

The Ten Maidens 25:1–13

The parable of the Ten Maidens (or Bridesmaids) is proper to Matthew (25:1–13). The introductory formula does not, of course, mean that the kingdom is directly compared to three maidens. It is shorthand for: "It is the case with the kingdom of heaven as with ten maidens…" The final coming of the kingdom may be likened to the whole situation about to be described. It would appear that the ten girls wait at the bridegroom's house to greet, formally, the bridegroom when he comes with his bride after a nighttime wedding. The cry "Lord, Lord" of the foolish ones (v. 11) echoes the "Lord, Lord" of 7:21—of those who are not doers of the word. And the reply of "the Lord" in each case is the same: "I never knew you" (7:23); "I do not know you" (25:12). The parable stresses constant watchfulness (even though all the girls fall asleep for a time, even those who are admitted to the wedding feast!). In a broader sense, it points to the seriousness of our relationship with God. This is something each person must possess for oneself; nobody else can fashion it for one. It is something each one must work at during one's lifetime; one cannot borrow it at the last moment. It is of vital importance, because it is really a statement of how one sees oneself and the meaning of one's life.

The Talents 25:14–30

In 25:1–13, Matthew dealt with the delay of the parousia (a parousia that will happen in its time, 24:48–51). Now he goes on to explain what it means to be watchful or ready during the delay (cf. Luke 19:11–27). It is to be faithful to the Lord's instructions and to carry them out, energetically, with all our God-given ability. We are not to sit back, with arms folded, quietly waiting for the Lord. The time of waiting is meant to be filled by our deeds of love.

The "talent" entrusted to the servants is the largest currency unit of the time. (Precisely because of this parable, the word "talent" has taken on its familiar metaphorical meaning.) The first two servants by industrious trading doubled the respective amounts received. The third man, a man afflicted with "prudence," carefully hid his money. With his "after a long time" (v. 19), Matthew denotes the delay of the parousia. The Lord, *ho kyrios*, or "master" has returned and held a reckoning. The first two servants are congratulated and rewarded for their enterprise and fidelity. The reward of faithful and profitable service is greater responsibility and acceptance into a more intimate relationship with the Lord. Though their responsibility had been unequal (five talents and two talents), their reward is the same (vv 21, 23). What matters is wholehearted commitment, not accomplishment.

The third servant receives blame and condemnation, because he had done nothing. He had been too "prudent" to take a risk. Punishment is for disuse rather than abuse of what had been entrusted. The servant's characterization of the master as "a hard man" betrays his manner of imaging God (quite like that of the elder son of Luke's parable: "all these years I have been working like a slave for you, and I have never disobeyed your command" (Luke 15:29). One who so images God will strive to live within "safe" legal parameters; will take no risk. The others had the confidence and the freedom to "trade" (vv. 16–17). Their God was not a "hard man."

Matthew would appear to be warning Christian leaders who portrayed God as an exacting taskmaster to the detriment of his loving Parenthood. The upshot is that the inactive servant loses everything. Likely, verse 29 was originally a cynical proverb to the effect that the rich get richer and the poor poorer. In its present context, it refers to the human response to God's gift. One who commits oneself will receive generously; one who is ungenerous and selfish will end up losing what little one has. The warning is clear: a Christian who will not "do" one's faith must face a bitter reckoning.

The Judgment 25:31–46

This is Matthew's great scene of the Last Judgment. In it the Son of Man is emphatically a king who sits in judgment. Perhaps largely through the influence of this passage, the image of Christ as judge has had a profound impact on Christian tradition. However, this image of Christ is far from being the dominant one in the New Testament. And, even in our passage, when one looks closely, it will be seen that the judgment is "auto-judgment": we judge ourselves by our omissions or our deeds. It is not so surprising that there has been concern with the King and the Judge: that drew attention from a disturbing factor. Properly understood, the parable is subversive of ecclesiastical systems; a denial of the label "Christian" to any church not characterized by loving concern for the poor. It underlines the fact that if Christ is king, his kingdom, his manner of kingship, is not of this world (see John 18:36).

In the parables of chapters 24—25, Matthew had summoned to watchfulness, to readiness, to faithfulness. Now, in 25:31–46, he spells out what it means to be watchful and ready and faithful. It means being able to recognize the Son of Man in all those in need, to be loving towards the Son of Man in those in need, to translate this love into deeds of concern. There is the yardstick, and by it one is measured. On performance of or neglect of these works of mercy hangs salvation.

To appreciate this passage rightly, one must understand that it is retrospective. Matthew has in mind how Jesus comported himself; how he related to people. What Jesus did and said becomes the standard of judgment. He had come, a human being, into our human history, to tell us of the Godness of God. Jesus taught and lived the truth that the reality of God is revealed in the realization of more humanity between fellow human beings: giving drink to the thirsty, feeding the hungry, welcoming the stranger. Matthew's story of judgment is focused on purely human concerns; and these are God's concern: "Come, you blessed of my Father." The emphasis is on the needy person, the one in distress. What is at stake in the last judgment is our attitude towards the little ones, the humble, and the needy. The criterion is not the standard of religion or cult. It is, starkly, whether one has helped those in need.

The scene is vivid. Mixed flocks of (white) sheep and (black) goats were a common sight in Palestine. Here sheep and goats separate for final blessing or curse. The king of the heavenly kingdom sits in judgment on his people. The good works of verses 34–36 are the traditional "corporal works of mercy" and the elect have performed these works. Their surprise, their amazement, is in being told by the king that they had been done "to me." Astounded, they ask: "When?...when?...when?" The answer is Jesus' solemn attestation of his total identification with the poor and outcast and oppressed. It might seem, at first sight, that this Matthean scene has nothing specifically Christian about it. However, when we realize that nothing less than the comportment of Jesus himself is the yardstick of judgment, we can see how thoroughly Christian it is. And this is so, even though it embraces "all the nations"—all people without distinction (v. 32).

The truth is that this king who is judge of all is the crucified king, and he is met in every one who suffers. It is because they had failed to understand Jesus' identification with the suffering that the "goats" had failed to minister to him and to serve him. They had not loved the poor in concrete deeds of mercy. This Jesus, the crucified one, is the Son of Man who utters judgment; but what kind of judgment is this? He is the one who identifies himself with the lowly—with all the daughters and sons of men. He is the loving and living expression of God's concern for humanity. A God bent on humankind, and nothing short of that, becomes the standard of our concern for those in need. That is why this concern alone is the criterion of judgment. That is why the words of warning sound so harshly: "Depart from me, you cursed."

Straightaway, a problem: Can one, as a Christian, really believe that the suffering Jesus on the cross, who in Luke's passion story prayed, "Father, forgive them, for they do not know what they are doing" (Luke 23:34), could, as risen Lord, declare in awful judgment: "Depart from me, you cursed, into the eternal fire"? Matthew, it seems (25:41), would have us think so. That such is really his intent becomes incredible when we understand that the "they" of Luke's text embraces all who brought Jesus to death. Jesus prays forgiveness for the obdurate chief priests and their allies. Luke is suggesting that even perpetrators of evil never really appreciate God's goodness or the strange wisdom of his purpose.

Besides, we should see that seeming irrevocable sentence against what we know of the God of the Old Testament and the New. He is the wondrously inconsistent God who "grieves to his heart" that he had ever made the complicated, stubborn, and treacherous human creature (Gen 6:5–8), only to decide to put up with them henceforth (Gen 8:1); she is the God whose mother-heart recoils at the prospect of losing Ephraim (Hosea 11:8); he is the God who desires the salvation of all (1 Tim 2:40); he is the God who did not spare his own Son (John 3:16). Surely, Jesus would have us believe that his God and ours loves us with divine love that is beyond our human imagining.

Still, what are we to make of Matthew's Last Judgment? We are to understand it as myth. Myth is a symbolic form of expression couched in narrative, which is not intended to be historical. It deals with realities that transcend experience—in this case, the reality of definitive encounter with God. Besides, there is the factor of Semitic rhetoric—an exaggerated statement for the sake of emphasis. We have met such statements: "If your hand or your foot causes you to stumble, cut it off and throw it away" (18:8). The strongest manner of highlighting a warning is to cast it in the form of an inflexible judgment. In effect, the "last judgment" is a warning; it primarily relates to one's conduct in the present. One is challenged to live in such a manner that, should the day of reckoning occur, one would not be caught unawares. We are being taught how we should prepare for the "coming" of the Lord, prepare for our meeting with him. The "last judgment" is taking place in my life here and now. The "books" are being written: human responsibility. But, has my name "been written in the book of life since the foundation of the world" (Rev 17:8)? There is the true judgment.

As a closing comment, a provocative word on the Matthean judgment scene:

> I believe—and I say it with some hesitation—that at the last judgment, perhaps everyone will stand at the right-hand side of the Son of Man. "Come all you beloved people, blessed of the Father, for despite all your inhumanity, you once gave a glass of water when I was in need. Come!"[1]

Does this seem outrageous? I do not think so. That man of Nazareth, who went about doing good, who died on a cross because he had espoused the cause of human freedom—he will not have us view God as an inflexible judge. He would have us see the tears of a God who weeps in concert with human woe.[2]

NOTES

1. Edward Schillebeeckx, *God Among Us* (New York: Crossroad, 1993), 62.
2. Wilfrid J. Harrington, *The Loving God* (Dublin: The Columba Press, 2012).

CHAPTER 9

THE PASSION, DEATH, AND RESURRECTION

And remember, I am with you always, to the end of the age.

Matthew 28:20

"When Jesus had finished saying all these things..." This phrase concludes each of the Sermons (see 7:28; 11:1; 13:53; 19:1; 26:1). Now there is an air of finality. The time of preaching is over; the mission is at an end. In Matthew, Jesus prophesies his passion: "You know that after two days the Passover is coming, and the Son of Man will be handed over to be crucified" (26:2; see Mark 14:1).

PLOT, ANOINTING, BETRAYAL 26:6–16

The sequel to the priests' plot to arrest Jesus by stealth (vv. 3–5) is obviously Judas' betrayal (vv. 14–16). The intercalated anointing scene (vv. 6–13) is thereby highlighted and is meant to be understood in the context of the framework. The woman doing the anointing is not named, nor those who object to her action. The interest falls on the words of Jesus (vv. 10–13). She had performed a good service, more significant than she knew. Anointing for burial was not her intent; it is how Jesus chose to view it. Her gesture, at the opening of the passion, points to the heart of the good news: salvation through the death of the Savior. Poignantly, the lovely deed of this unknown woman stands between the deadly intent of the priests and the betrayal of Jesus by a disciple.

PASSION AND DEATH 26:36—27:66

In his Passion Narrative, Matthew has followed Mark quite closely. Both Gospels present a Jesus who is abandoned by his followers and who has to face his hour alone. Both have a Jewish and a Roman trial of Jesus. The Jewish authorities try to convict Jesus of planning to destroy the Temple. When he acknowledges that he is the Messiah, the Son of God, he is accused of blasphemy. The Roman trial centers on Jesus' claim of being the king of the Jews. While Pilate knows that Jesus is a just man, he hands him over to be crucified. Both authorities fail to grant Jesus justice and both maltreat him. There is no friend or supporter by the cross; Jesus was rejected and mocked.

Two prayers frame the journey to the cross. At the beginning, in Gethsemane, Jesus prays to his Abba-Father to let the cup pass from him. At the end, at Golgotha, he prays to "my God," asking why he has been forsaken. He dies with an anguished cry, seemingly wholly defeated. If Jesus' prayer had gone unanswered, his God had not been absent at all. As Raymond Brown described,

> In their Passion Narrative Mark/Matthew dramatize how difficult it is for Jesus to go through his crucifixion and how he is clearly recognized as belonging to God only after he has suffered to the full. This is meant both as a graphic warning and a consolation to the readers of these Gospels. If the Master found it difficult, if the closest disciples all failed to follow Jesus in bearing the cross, the readers too will find it difficult and will flee. Yet the God who vindicated Jesus, though at times seeming to have forsaken them, will ultimately be their vindicator as well when their final hour has come and their Golgotha looms before them, if like them they have the courage to say "let us go."[1]

While the Passion Narratives of Mark and Matthew are remarkably close, there are still significant differences. Here we will concentrate on the distinctive elements of the Matthean narrative.[2]

Special Matthean Passion Material

1. The Death of Judas 27:3–10
2. The Dream of Pilate's Wife 27:19
3. Pilate Washes His Hands 27:24–25

4. A Popular Poetic Quatrain 27:51b–53

5. The Guard-at-the-Tomb 27:62–66; 28:2–4, 11–15

Brown finds, in the special material Matthew has grouped around the birth and death of Jesus, a consistency that points to a source—a "popular" source. He discerns in this special material a strongly anti-Jewish character. The Jewish authorities seem notably malevolent. Even the Jewish crowd is emphatically antagonistic. The Jewish nation had brought upon itself the divine punishment, which, in the Jewish Christian view (and Matthew is a Jewish Christian Gospel), found expression in the destruction of Jerusalem and its Temple. "Such broad polemics against 'the Jews'... go beyond what is found in the body of Matthew's Gospel. In my opinion they reflect the unnuanced, prejudiced theological judgments found among the ordinary people who are the source of the stories that make up the Matthean special material."[3]

The major Matthean difference from Mark is the introduction of responsibility for the death of Jesus. In Old Testament terms, it is presented as guilt of the blood of an innocent person wrongfully condemned to death. This emerges in scenes peculiar to Matthew. Judas tries to shake off his responsibility; the chief priests seek to rid themselves of the "blood money"; Pilate's wife warns her husband to extricate himself from his involvement with this just man; Pilate washes his hands. No attempt succeeds; all are tainted by their part in betraying innocent blood.

MATTHEAN MODIFICATIONS

In a lead-up to a consideration of the special Matthean material, it will help to note a few passages where Matthew has made significant additions to Mark's text.

Gethsemane

Matthew 26:42—Matthew has expanded Mark 14:39 into a second prayer of Jesus: "My Father, if this cannot pass unless I drink it, your will be done."

26:49—"Greetings, Rabbi!" Jesus does not approve of the use of "rabbi" as a salutation (much less as a title). Judas' use of the term (vv. 22, 25) marks him as one already outside the company of Jesus' disciples.

26:51–54—Matthew specifies that he who cut off the ear of the high priest's slave was "one of those with Jesus." See Mark 14:47—"one of those who stood near." Matthew, unlike Mark, records Jesus' response to the sword-wielder (vv. 52–54). The command to put up the sword is bolstered by a warning. Besides, Jesus does not need such paltry help: his Father could readily supply "more than twelve legions of angels." See Dan 12:1; 2 Macc 5:2–3; 10:29–30. The scriptures must be fulfilled (vv. 54, 56)—see Matthew 26:31 (Zech 13:7); and 27:46 (Ps 22:2). In Matthew's view God has written from beginning to end what must be.

26:59—All the Gospels agree that the Sanhedrin authorities were instrumental in having Jesus arrested and in handing him over to the Romans for sentence of death. However, Matthew emphasizes the malevolence of Jewish involvement. In Matthew 26:69, the "chief priests and the whole council" seek *false* testimony against Jesus (cf. Mark 14:55). It is probable that something said or done by Jesus had been interpreted as a threat to destroy the Temple and would have been a partial cause of the Sanhedrin's action against Jesus. But Matthew is proposing conscious vindictiveness.

The Price of Innocent Blood 27:3–10

In 27:1–2, Matthew tells of Jesus being led to Pilate. Then follows the first of the passages peculiarly his own: Judas and the price of innocent blood (27:3–10). When Judas had agreed to betray Jesus, he had received in payment thirty pieces of silver (26:14–15). Now, full of remorse, he comes back with the money: "I have sinned by betraying innocent blood" (27:3–4). He is conscious of a heinous crime (see Jer 26:15; 2 Kgs 24:4). The priests respond callously, "What is that to us?" A despairing Judas throws the money into the Temple sanctuary and goes and hangs himself—an action reminiscent of Ahitophel (2 Sam 17:23). The high priests, like it or not, are contaminated by the blood money. Their decision to be rid of it is indirect acknowledgment of Jesus' innocence: "It is not lawful to put them in the treasury, since they are blood money" (v. 6), with "blood money" being the price of innocent blood. The passage ends with the purchase of the Field of Blood (vv. 7–8) and a typical Matthean fulfillment citation, this one rather obscure (vv. 9–10). Another, notably different version of the fate of Judas is found in Acts 1:16–20. Evidently, there was an early Christian tradition about the sudden death of Judas, or, perhaps, a conviction that he must have come to a sticky end.[4]

The Roman Trial 27:1–26

Matthew's Roman trial is twice as long as the Markan account. Matthew followed Mark but supplemented the material with further dramatic incidents that enliven the account and heighten the theological import. In the Barabbas incident (27:15–16), some manuscripts are intriguing: "At that time they had a notorious prisoner, called *Jesus* Barabbas. So after they had gathered, Pilate said to them, 'Whom do you want me to release for you, *Jesus* Barabbas or Jesus who is called the Messiah?'" The reading Jesus Barabbas is now widely regarded as authentic, as in the NRSV. A weighty argument is that, while it is easy to imagine Christian scribes wanting to omit that embarrassing "Jesus," it is incomprehensible that they should have added it. The Matthean contrast is highly dramatic.

The message of Pilate's wife (v. 19) is proper to Matthew: "While he was sitting on the judgment seat, his wife sent word to him, 'Have nothing to do with that innocent man, for today I have suffered a great deal because of a dream about him.'" This connects with the Judas story ("innocent blood," "innocent man") and leads to the episode of Pilate's hand-washing. Indeed, it was his wife's testimony that led Pilate to strive to avoid the taint of innocent blood. The dream motif recalls the dreams of Joseph (1:20; 2:13, 19) and of the magi (2:12) in the infancy narrative.

In Matthew 27:23, Pilate declares the innocence of Jesus—as he does three times in Luke and John. This leads to another episode proper to Matthew where Pilate washes his hands (vv. 24–25: "He took some water and washed his hands before the crowd saying, 'I am innocent of this man's blood; see to it yourselves.'" The background is Deuteronomy 21:1–9—hardly a passage that Pilate would have read! There have been, then, three attempts to evade responsibility for the innocent blood of Jesus. (What is in question is the responsibility implied in the storyline, not the actual guilt of those involved.)

Despite his gesture with the money, Judas could not escape guilt for having set in motion a destructive process that could not be reversed. God's punishment for that guilt was evidenced in Judas' suicide. (This again is the popular estimation). Although the chief priests, by rejecting the return of the money, tried to escape Judas' transfer of responsibility to them, they were the most responsible for innocent blood because of the death sentence they had just passed on Jesus, after having sought false testimony against him (26:59, 66). Jesus had warned that divine judgment would come upon them (26:64). As for Pilate's attempt to avoid responsibility while passing sentence of death on an innocent man, the washing ritual of Deuteronomy 21 is efficacious only if the elders who performed it had no share in the murder either by doing it themselves or knowing who did. Pilate may not have borne the principal responsibility, but he cannot wash himself free of guilt.

His Blood Be Upon Us! 27:25

Matthew adds a response to that gesture of Pilate: "Then the people as a whole answered, 'His blood be on us and on our children!'" (27:25). Using a well-known biblical formula (cf. Lev 2:9–15; Josh 2:19–20; 2 Sam 1:16; 14:9; Jer 51:35), the people accept responsibility for Jesus' death. Pilate has (to his satisfaction) waived responsibility. He challenged the crowd: "See to it yourselves." In other words, you shoulder the blame. Convinced that Jesus, who had been condemned by the Sanhedrin (for them, the religious authority), was a blasphemer, they do accept responsibility. They act on their discernment of the situation. The phrase, "and our children," in context means one generation involving the destruction of Jerusalem and the Temple (see Matt 24:15–21). Historically, this text has had dire consequences for Jews. The comment of Daniel Harrington is apposite:

> Matthew 27:11–26 (and especially 27:25) is a major text in the history and present reality of Christian-Jewish relations. Teachers and preachers have a serious obligation to work through this text with care and objectivity. They must give attention to the conflicting portraits of Pilate in the Gospels and other Jewish sources. They must help others to see Matthew's special interest in the Jewish leaders and crowds and his comparative lack of interest in

> Pilate. Above all it is necessary to read Matt 27:25 ("His blood be upon us and upon our children") in its Matthean setting, not as applying to all Jews at all times or just the small percentage of Jews in Jerusalem who involved themselves in Jesus' trial before Pilate. The Matthean setting involves both the time of Jesus and the time after 70 A.D., and is rooted in an inner-Jewish quarrel.[5]

Apocalyptic Signs 27:51b–53

The death of Jesus was followed by the rending of the curtain of the temple, signaling the end of the temple, or even of the Old Covenant (27:51a). Here, Matthew adds four apocalyptic signs: "The earth shook and the rocks were split. The tombs also were opened, and many bodies of the saints who had fallen asleep were raised. After his resurrection they came out of the tombs and entered the holy city and appeared to many" (vv. 51b–53). The whole passage is symbolic and couched in popular poetic terms. The "earthquake" marks the death of Jesus as an epoch-making event and serves as a prelude to the resurrection of the dead. The rising of "many bodies" is not the general resurrection. It is symbolic of the breaking in of God's power, signaling the beginning of the last era, and it characterizes the death/resurrection of Jesus as an event that makes possible the resurrection of others. "After his resurrection" is awkward in its setting. (Tombs opened at the death of Jesus but the raised appeared only after Jesus' resurrection.) Its purpose is theological: to link the resurrection of the "saints" with the resurrection of Jesus (and not only with his death). One asks of the passage: What does it mean? not, did all this happen?

RESURRECTION 28:1–15

When, in 1 Corinthians 15, Paul energetically defends the reality of resurrection from the dead, he starts by appealing to the resurrection of Jesus (15:3–8). It is clear, from the New Testament that Christians were, from the outset, convinced that the crucified Christ was not held by death. In Jewish faith and prayer, God is he who "makes the dead live." Jewish faith and hope looked to a resurrection of the righteous at the end of time. The first Christians asserted that, in the person of Jesus of Nazareth, this divine act had taken place. Jewish expectation was eschatological: resurrection was an event of the end-time. Christians were asserting that an eschatological event had taken place in time. If one may put it so, the resurrection of Jesus is an event at once eschatological and historical. In essence, it is a spiritual event beyond our world of time, and yet it has impinged on our world of time. Paul uses the word *ophthe* to state that Christ appeared to Cephas, to the other witnesses listed, and to Paul himself. The word can be rendered "he showed himself." It means that the risen Jesus manifested himself as present in some fashion so that Paul, and the others, can say, "I have seen the Lord." A divine initiative leads to real experience of the presence of the Lord and a firm conviction of the reality of this presence. Something had happened to these men and women that they could only describe by saying that they had "seen the Lord," that the Lord had "shown himself" to them. The phrase did not refer to some general Christian experience, but rather to a particular series of occurrences confined to a limited period. Such occurrences, on the threshold of ordinary human experience, would simply not submit to precision of detail. Only symbol and imagery, not literal prose, could tell *this* story. The evangelists can write of the death of Jesus—death we recognize. But there is no attempt to relate the wholly mysterious fact of his being raised from death.

The Narratives

Six Gospel passages serve as sources for our knowledge of the resurrection: Mark 16:1–8; Matthew 28; Luke 24:13–49; John 20; John 21; Mark 16:9–20 (and to these should be added Paul's text in 1 Cor 15:5–8). In this group we may distinguish two types of narrative: those of the post-resurrection appearances, and those of the finding of the empty tomb. The narratives of the post-resurrection appearances were composed to ground Christian faith in the risen Jesus and to justify apostolic preaching. The nature of such appearances makes it obvious that the Gospels cannot agree where and to whom Jesus appeared. This diversity does not seriously affect the historicity of the occurrences; it is a product of the manner in which the stories were told and preserved. A constant feature of the resurrection narratives, with the exception of Matthew 28 (but note 28:17) is that the Lord is not at once recognized (Luke 24:16, 37; John 20:14–15; 21; 4). It required some word or some familiar gesture of his to make him known. This is an effective way of making the point that Jesus had not returned to life as before but had passed beyond death to *new* life with God. He is Jesus—and yet is different. The appearance stories are heavily laden with theological and apologetic motifs.

The Empty Tomb 28:1–15

The women (Matt 28:1) came to "see" the tomb (and not to anoint the body of Jesus as in Mark 16:1). Here that office is ruled out because of the guard at the tomb. The apocalyptic "earthquake" (v. 2) links the resurrection with the death (27:51–54) as the great eschatological event that ushers in the new age. The "guards" (v. 4) are those of 27:62–66, a passage that is a product of Christian apologetic concern. The interpreting angel addressed his glad tidings to the women: they must not fear but should rejoice because the crucified Jesus they sought has been raised. With joy, they ran to tell the disciples (effectively, the Twelve). Suddenly, Jesus met them. Here, uniquely in stories of encounter with the risen Jesus, he is recognized at once. Fittingly, the women worship this Lord. His message was that they must hasten to announce the good news to the disciples: they will meet Jesus again in Galilee. Go and tell "my *brothers*," those who had failed him so miserably. It is the graciousness of total forgiveness. The word of God is for all ages; there is surely a message for our day in this passage. *Women* were the first to hear the good news of the resurrection; *women* were the first heralds of the resurrection (vv. 7, 10). *Women* were the first to meet the risen Lord, or rather, to be met by him! When will the Church hearken to this word?

The final Matthean special material is that which specifies guards at the tomb (27:62–66). Matthew's purpose is polemical: to refute a current story that Jesus' disciples had stolen the body and on that basis had proclaimed the resurrection. While it continues into the empty tomb narrative (28:2–4, 11–15), comparison with the other Gospels makes clear that the guard story is not historical. After recounting that the guards had been bribed to spread the story that the disciples had stolen the body of Jesus, Matthew observes: "this story is still told among the Jews to this day" (28:15). The episode has been built into the burial and empty tomb stories as a way of anticipating an objection that is sure to be raised. Christians knew that the tomb was found empty, not because the body had been stolen, but because Jesus had been raised from the dead. But that tiresome objection had to be met and a lie nailed.

The Lord of Life

It is evident from our Gospels that the resurrection of Jesus is not at all the resuscitation of a corpse in the sense of a return to earthly life. The resurrection of Jesus means his rising to life beyond death. The risen Jesus lives a life that transcends earthly life; he has broken out of the confines of time and place. The risen Jesus was present to his disciples in a new and unfettered manner, and not only to his original disciples. He is present, potentially, to all men and women through time and history. This abiding presence is implied in Matthew 28:20: "I am with you always, to the end of the age." He is the same Jesus of his earthly life, but now transformed. Paul can declare: "The last Adam [Christ] became a life-giving Spirit" (1 Cor 15:45), living a Spirit-life now and no longer a life of flesh. Christians came to understand that "eternal life" is life with God and with the risen Jesus. That conviction is enshrined in the promise to the "good thief": "Truly I tell you, today you will be with me in paradise" (Luke 23:43). Instead of trying to situate or describe "paradise," it is more profitable to recall the comment of Ambrose: *Vita est enim esse cum Christo: ideo ubi Christus, ibi vita, ibi regnum*; "Life means living with Christ. Where Christ is, there too is life and there is the kingdom."

The Great Commission 28:16–20

The disciples went to Galilee as they had been bidden (28:10). There the risen Jesus appeared to them. A "mountain" is a place of revelation—an apt setting. The "eleven" adored their Lord, yet some "doubted." Matthew is drawing for his community a picture of the Christian community: believers caught between adoration and doubt. Jesus solemnly proclaimed that by his death-resurrection he had been granted what had been declared of the Son of Man in Daniel 7:14: "To him was given dominion and glory and kingship, that all peoples, nations and languages should serve him." (cf. Matt 28:18). He was therefore in a position to launch a universal mission. He duly commissioned his representatives who were to achieve his task. Consequently, he sends them into the world to make disciples of "all nations." During his ministry, Jesus limited his concern to Israel; in this new era the good news is for *all*.

One becomes a *disciple* through baptism "in the name of the Father and of the Son and of the Holy Spirit;" a triadic formula that doubtless comes from the baptismal liturgy of Matthew's community. The disciples are to teach: to carry on what was a major task of the earthly Jesus in the Gospel. Disciples must be taught *Jesus'* commands: "these words of mine" (7:24, 26). Christians do not live by the Ten Commandments—even though Jesus' teaching includes much of what was in Torah. For the Christian, Jesus' word is the ultimate norm of morality. In that word one will discern the will of God.

Finally, we have Jesus' great promise of v. 20b: "And remember, I am with you always, to the end of the age." Matthew skillfully rounds off his Gospel by catching up the Emmanuel (God-with-us) of his prologue (1:23). Matthew does not speak of a "departure" or of a "farewell" of Jesus. Rather, he places the community at the heart of the universal power of the resurrection. The "end of the age" that he has in mind designates the time of the church (see 13:39–40; 24:3). It corresponds to the "from now on" of 26:64 where Jesus tells Caiaphas: "From now on you will see the Son of man seated at the right hand of Power." Jesus is promising his steadfast help, echoing all his assurances throughout the Gospel: Fear not!; I am with you!; It is I! Whereas Luke closes with a farewell blessing and ascension (Luke 24:51), in Matthew, Jesus assures us that he will be abidingly present in the community. Moreover, what is present is not his static presence in one chosen group, but his dynamic and helping presence for a worldwide mission. This promise to be with us always is an encouraging word to the Church of our day—a Church seemingly lost in a mass of humanity. As Donald Senior describes,

> The story concludes on a mountain in Galilee with the gospel turning its face to the future and to the nations. But in a very real sense, it does not conclude at all. Through the final words of Jesus to his disciples, Matthew projects the gospel story out into the time and space of the reader's world, and even farther, to those who would accept the message of Jesus' missionaries, be baptized by them, and through them be schooled in the way of Jesus. Jesus' message to the disciples is now clearly a message directed to the church.[6]

NOTES

1. Raymond E. Brown, *The Death of the Messiah*, 2 vols. (New York: Doubleday, 1994), 27f.

2. Here I follow the relevant lines of R. E. Brown's investigation in *The Death of the Messiah*.

3. Brown, *Death of the Messiah,* 68.

4. For the New Testament picture of Judas, see Wilfrid J. Harrington, *From the Presence of the Lord: A God Too Gracious* (Dublin: The Columba Press, 2006), 55–64.

5. Daniel J. Harrington, SJ, *Matthew*. Sacra Pagina 1. A Michael Glazier Book (Collegeville, MN: The Liturgical Press, 1991), 393.

6. Donald Senior, *The Gospel of Matthew* (Nashville: Abingdon Press, 1997), 177.

Epilogue

Jesus of Nazareth is one. Christian perception of him varies. The variation is manifest in the Gospels. While the works of Mark, Matthew, and Luke are closely related, the differences are manifest. These are, in large measure, occasioned by the community situation of each evangelist and by the concerns and needs of that situation. The temperament of each is surely also a factor. Matthew's community was Jewish-Christian. In the stressful days after the traumatic disaster of AD 70, it found itself in a state of cold war with official Judaism. Its stance was that Jesus is the Teacher who speaks more authoritatively than Moses. This is stressed by Matthew. Arguably, the statement, "Every scribe who has been trained for the kingdom of heaven is like the master of a household who brings out of his treasures what is new and what is old" (13:52), reflects Matthew's view of himself as something of a Christian sage. At any rate, in his Sermons, he has cast Jesus as the Sage.

Beforehand, in his Infancy Narrative, he firmly asserted that Jesus is Son of David and Son of Abraham: Savior of Jew and Gentile. At the same time, his ancestry shows him to be wholly one of us, "like his brothers and sisters in every respect" (Heb 2:17). Virginally conceived, Jesus is God-with-us. Son of David, he was, appropriately, born in Bethlehem. The Gentile Magi acknowledged the king of the Jews. He reenacted the exodus of his people and, figuratively, suffered their exile. As "the Nazarene" he embarked on his mission. The Sermons follow the stages of the mission.

In the Sermon on the Mount, Jesus addressed his people; the beatitudes are thoroughly Jewish in form and content. He assured his people that he had not come to abolish the Torah and Prophets; he was their prophetic fulfillment. His challenge broadened and deepened the meaning of the term "righteousness," the doing of God's will. For the Christian, the ultimate authority is not the Law of Moses but "these words of mine."

Jesus was sent "only to the lost sheep of the house of Israel." The initial mission of the Twelve had the same limitation. Matthew's community saw itself as the authentic way of Judaism. Mission brings trial. They must maintain trust in God. They, and those who hearkened to them, will be recompensed by a generous God. Jesus spoke in parables. His purpose was unequivocal: to challenge and teach. Matthew, in the Sermon in Parables, gives the impression that Jesus was reacting to the rejection of his word: his parables were punishment for disbelief. Again, the evangelist displays his preoccupation: the struggle with contemporary Judaism.

Paradoxically, in 13:36–52, Jesus encourages his disciples—in parables.

A Christian community needs structure, but there is inherent danger. This is brought out in the Sermon on the Church (chapter 18). It is the special duty of leaders to care for the weak and vulnerable; not, through insensitivity, to make their lot harder. All members of a community should display mutual concern, especially where there is need of correction. Forgiveness—"seventy times seven"—is the hallmark. They are to mirror the conduct of an infinitely forgiving Abba. As for the exercise of authority, chapter 23 shows, eloquently, how it is *not* to be exercised. Jesus had stood authority on its head: *exousia* (authority) is shown in *diakonia* (service). Already, by Matthew's time, Christian leaders were sporting titles and flexing ecclesiastical muscle.

The Judgment Sermon (chapters 24—25) uses the prospect of eschatological trials to exhort Christians to respond to present difficulties. Parables figure prominently. The Ten Maidens parable inculcates watchfulness. The Talents parable challenges an image of God as an exacting taskmaster who inhibits. The image of a generous God is liberating; one will dare to take risks. The Last Judgment serves as an imperative call to action in the here and now. Jesus' solidarity with all who suffer seals his image of the gracious God who has a preferential option for the poor.

In his Passion, Jesus, abandoned by his followers, faced his hour of trial alone. In Gethsemane he suffered the pain of unanswered prayer; on Calvary, the anguish of God-forsakenness. All evangelists stress the innocence of Jesus and have Pilate witness to it. Matthew underlines the fact by presenting the death of Jesus as the heinous crime of the shedding of innocent blood. This is acknowledged by Judas and the priests and, dramatically, by Pilate in his futile washing of hands. The Magi had come to seek "the king of the Jews." Jesus died as King of the Jews. The further significance of his death was marked, symbolically, by apocalyptic signs. The centurion and his men confessed in awe: "Truly this man was God's Son!"

Death was not the end. The women, who had come to mourn a dead Jesus, were met by the risen Lord. He gave them a message for his "brothers:" their failure forgiven. They will see Jesus in Galilee, and when they met him, they received the commission: "Go therefore and make disciples of all nations." And the assurance: "And remember, I am with you always, to the end of the age."

Select Bibliography

General

Brown, R. E. *The Birth of the Messiah.* Updated ed. New York: Doubleday, 1993.

———. *The Death of the Messiah.* 2 vols. New York: Doubleday, 1994.

Dunn, J. D. G. *Jesus Remembered.* Grand Rapids, Michigan: Eerdmans, 2003.

Meier, J. P. *A Marginal Jew: Rethinking the Historical Jesus, Vol I.* New York: Doubleday. 1991.

Pagola, J. A. *Jesus: An Historical Approximation.* Miami: Convivium Press, 2012.

Sanders, E. P. *Jesus and Judaism.* London: SCM, 1985.

———. *The Historical Figure of Jesus.* London: Penguin Books, 1995.

Matthew

Beare, F. W. *The Gospel According to Matthew.* San Francisco: Harper & Row, 1981.

Brown, R. E. "The Gospel According to Matthew." In *An Introduction to the New Testament*, 171–227. New York: Doubleday, 1997.

Davies, W. D. and D. C. Allison. *The Gospel According to St Matthew*. ICC. 3 vols. Edinburgh: T. & T. Clark, 1988.

Harrington, D. J. *The Gospel of Matthew*. Sacra Pagina I. A Michael Glazier Book. Collegeville: The Liturgical Press, 1991.

Harrington, W. J. *Matthew: Sage Theologian*. Dublin: The Columba Press, 1998.

Kingsbury, J. D. *Matthew: Structure, Christology, Kingdom*. Philadelphia: Fortress, 1975.

———. *Matthew as Story*. Philadelphia: Fortress, 1988.

Meier, J. P. *Matthew*. New Testament Message 3. Wilmington: Michael Glazier, 1980.

———. *The Vision of Matthew: Christ, Church, and Morality in the First Gospel*. New York: Crossword, 1991.

Powell, M. A., D. R. Bauer, K. R. Snodgrass et al. "The Gospel of Matthew." *Interpretation* 46, no. 4 (1992).

Senior, D. *The Gospel of Matthew*. Nashville: Abingdon Press, 1997.

Stanton, G. N. *A Gospel for a New People. Studies in Matthew*. Edinburgh: T. & T. Clark, 1992.

Stock, A. *The Method and Message of Matthew*. Collegeville: The Liturgical Press, 1994.

GLOSSARY

It is my hope that this glossary will provide the reader the meaning of some recurring terms that appear in the text.

Allegory - Allegory, in which the details of a story have symbolic value, such as in the Parable of the Wicked Tenants (Matthew 21:33-41), is extended metaphor and, as such, is a story that has both a literal and a metaphorical level. An allegorical story can well be a parable, as in the example cited. There are several allegorical parables in the Gospels.

Apocalyptic - "Apocalypse," from the Greek *apocalypsis* ("revelation"), designates a type of Jewish literature that flourished from about 200 BC to AD 100. As a literary form it is presented as a revelation, or series of revelations, of heavenly secrets made to a seer and conveyed in highly symbolic imagery. It is crisis literature. The biblical apocalypses are the Book of Daniel (more precisely, Daniel 7—12) and the Book of Revelation of John. Apocalypticism is the worldview of an apocalyptic movement. In this view it is taken for granted that a supernatural world stands above our earthly world. That heavenly world is the "real" world. There is a twofold dualism: vertical, the world above and our world, and horizontal, our age and the age to come. There is always a definitive eschatological judgment: the final clash between good and evil, issuing in the total victory of God and the end of evil. Apocalyptic ideas pervade the New Testament.

Apostle - The Christian mission was carried out by "apostles"—those "sent out" (*apostellein*) from the Christian communities.

Acts 13:1–4, the designation and sending out by the Antioch community of Barnabas and Saul, is an eloquent instance of this. There has been an unfortunate confusion of "Twelve" and "apostle." The Twelve were "apostles" in the sense that they had been "sent out" by Jesus. However, "apostle" has a much wider range than the Twelve.

Christology - Christology is the theological understanding of Jesus. In Jesus of Nazareth, God is really and truly present. That is the great Christian truth. However, to seek to define the mysterious nature of Jesus is a precarious endeavor. For centuries it has been assumed that the fifth-century Council of Chalcedon had spoken the definitive Christological word when it answered, in the affirmative, the question of whether God's salvation had been given, once and for all, in the man Jesus. Because the answer had to be Yes, and because salvation is of God, it had to be asserted, in the theological language of the day, that God himself was present in the man Jesus. That had been said, long before, by Paul: "God was in Christ, reconciling the world to himself" (2 Corinthians 11:25).

Covenant - Originally a treaty graciously "granted" by an overlord. God gave a covenant to his people at Sinai ("I am your God; you are my people") sealed and ratified in the blood of a sacrificial victim. Jeremiah spoke of a "new covenant" (Jeremiah 31:31–34). This new covenant with the new people of God was given through Jesus and sealed in his blood (see 1 Corinthians 11:25).

Disciple - Jesus gathered around himself a group of committed disciples, some of whom were also active in the early church. Distinctive features of this initial discipleship were: Jesus took the initiative in calling; "following" meant literal, physical following of an itinerant preacher, and disciples were warned that they might face suffering and hostility. The evidence is clear that some women did follow Jesus during his ministry in Galilee and accompanied him on his last journey to Jerusalem (see Matthew 12:46–50). "Disciple" is an inclusive term.

Eschatological - Pertaining to the *eschaton*, the End. Eschatology refers to the new age, the transformation of our world. But, with the coming of Jesus, this new age has already begun; we await the consummation. In the preaching of Jesus, the kingdom of God is eschatological: The definitive intervention of God, his kingly reign, is (in Jesus) a present reality. It seems that Jesus thought of himself as the eschatological prophet.

Kerygma - The "heralding" or "preaching" of the good news: the missionary preaching of the good news to Jews and Gentiles.

Kingdom of God - The precise phrase ***kingdom of God*** occurs only once in the Old Testament, in Wisdom 10:10. The expression was not current in Judaism at the time of Jesus and was not widely used by early Christians. "Kingdom of God" is found predominantly in the Synoptic Gospels (Matthew, Mark, and Luke) and then almost always on the lips of Jesus. It was evidently central to Jesus' proclamation. Israel regarded God as universal king. Furthermore, there was the expectation that God's reign would soon be manifested over the whole world. Jesus spoke mainly of a future kingdom: God will reveal himself in power and glory. There is evidence that Jesus also spoke of the kingdom as in some way already present in his own words and deeds. When we consider that the kingdom of God is not primarily a state or place, but rather the dynamic event of God coming in power to rule his people Israel in the end-time, it is not surprising that the precise relationship between the future and present kingdom is not specified. That is why Jesus can speak of the kingdom as both imminent and yet present. The important point is that Jesus deliberately chose to proclaim that the display of miraculous power throughout his ministry was a preliminary and partial realization of God's kingly rule.

Messiah - From a Hebrew Word meaning "anointed." In Greek it is rendered *Christos*, whence "Christ." In Jewish expectation, the Messiah would be God's instrument (not a divine figure) in ushering in his kingdom. The expectation is a development of the promise to David in 2 Samuel 7:11–16—the expectation of a royal Messiah. In the New Testament, Jesus is "son of David." It is unlikely that Jesus himself ever claimed to be the Messiah. It is also very likely that Jesus' opponents may have understood him and his followers to claim that he was the Messiah. After the resurrection, of course, Jesus was, by his followers, regularly called the Messiah—Jesus Christ (Messiah). But he was a paradoxical Messiah: one who suffered and died on a cross, not the triumphalist royal messiah of popular expectation.

Parable - A parable is a brief story with two levels of meaning. For instance, at first sight, the Sower looks like an agricultural vignette. Its true meaning has to do with reception of the gospel message. The second level of meaning is always the essential one. The purpose of a parable is to challenge decision and invite action.

Parousia - The Greek word *parousia* means "presence" or "arrival." In the ancient Greek-speaking world it was used of the ceremonial visit of a ruler or of the apparition of a god. In the New Testament, it is used of the "appearance" or coming of the glorified Christ at the close of salvation history. It expresses, in dramatic fashion, faith in a final act of God, marking the goal of human history and the establishment, in its fullness, of the kingdom of God. After New Testament times this came to be known, somewhat unhelpfully, as the Second Coming of Christ. The earliest Christians expected this consummation in their own time. The expectation may be, and is, often present without use of the term *parousia*.

Pharisees - The Pharisees formed a religious and political grouping of devout Jews that emphasized detailed study and observance of the Law of Moses. They also possessed a normative in judicial and religious proceedings in the Sanhedrin. They would have played a secretarial role and, as in modern civil service, some might have had a measure of influence. On the whole, they were "retainers." The Gospels seem to suggest that the scribes, as a homogenous group, formed part of a united front against Jesus. This is not historically accurate.

Sadducees - The Sadducees were a small group of priestly and lay aristocrats based in Jerusalem. They were theologically conservative, adhering to the clear teaching of the Torah, or Pentateuch (see Acts 26:6–10). The Sadducees appear rarely in the Synoptics and are completely absent from the writings of John and Paul.

Son of God - The New Testament church confessed Jesus as Son of God, and in doing so attributed to Jesus a unique relationship to God. Was the title *Son of God* bestowed on Jesus during his lifetime? In Matthew, it was used by Peter, in association with *Messiah* (16:16), and by the centurion (27:54). Jesus did not refer to himself directly as Son of God.

Son of Man - "The Son of Man" occurs more than eighty times in the Gospels and, practically without exception, as a self-designation by Jesus. Jesus used the phrase in a neutral sense to refer to himself indirectly. He likely had in mind as well the "one like a son of man" of Daniel 7:13. Jesus was the human one, serving God's purpose, and looking to vindication at the completion of his mission. Early Christians embraced the phrase, now regarded as a title.

Torah - Commonly translated "Law," but better rendered "instruction" or "guide of life," the Torah is basically the Pentateuch, the first five books of the Old Testament. For the Jews, the Torah was the full expression of God's purpose for his people. Indeed, Law and Lawgiver were practically identical. In this situation, the Torah took on an absolute value, and one could concern oneself exclusively with the law. This was an attitude combated by Jesus, notably in Matthew 5:17–20.

body of tradition—the traditions of the "fathers" or "elders." While they acknowledged that some of these legal rules and practices went beyond the Law, they maintained that such practices were, nevertheless, God's will for Israel. They actively engaged in trying to convince ordinary Jews to observe these practices in their daily life. Much of what is attributed to Pharisaic teaching refers to legal rulings or opinions regarding concrete behavior (*halakoth*) in matters of purity rules, Sabbath observance, tithing, marriage, and divorce. The Pharisees lacked political power but would have had some political influence. As a major religious force, they enjoyed the respect of the people. After AD 70 and the destruction of the Jerusalem Temple by the Romans, as practically the only religious group to have survived the Jewish War, their influence would have increased. All four Gospels attest to frequent contact of Jesus with Pharisees throughout his ministry. Not surprisingly, this relationship was one of tension because he and they addressed the same constituency. Jesus would have challenged them directly and in parable. Yet, the Gospels acknowledge that some Pharisees were willing to give Jesus a serious hearing (see, for example, Luke 7:36–50; John 3:1–2). It is noteworthy that Pharisees are practically absent in all Gospel passion narratives. The death of Jesus was brought about historically not by Pharisees, but by a religious and political alliance of Jerusalem priesthood and Roman political authority.

Pronouncement story - This is a brief story leading to a notable saying of Jesus; the story is designed to focus on the "punch line." For example, in Matthew 22:15–22 the saying "Give therefore to the emperor the things that are the emperor's, and to God the things that are God's" is effectively emphasized.

Scribes - The word *scribe* in Hebrew, Greek, and other languages had a wide range of meaning. Scribes wrote, copied, and guarded records for tax and military purposes, annals for government archives, and religious texts. Palestinian scribes in Jesus' time were, in fact, bureaucrats. In Jerusalem they assisted the priests